Abundance of Rain

Esther C. Stanley

Abundance of Rain
by Esther C. Stanley

Printed in the United States of America
ISBN 1-931232-64-4

Take note that satan and related names are not capitalised. I choose not to acknowledge God's enemy even to the extent of violating grammar rules.

Xulon Press
344 Maple Ave. West, #302
Vienna, VA 22180
703-691-7595
XulonPress.com

Dedicated to:

The Lord Jesus Christ,

Wonderful Counselor, Author and Friend;
Who commissioned me to write.

and to:

The Everlasting Father

Who has patiently loved me through each step
of the journey without judging;

and to:

Chinese Intercessors

who take up the responsibility of prayer for China,
the land of their God-given sovereignty.

"Of the increase of his government and peace there shall be no end, upon the throne of David, and upon his kingdom, to order it, and to establish it with judgment and with justice from henceforth even for ever. The zeal of the Lord of hosts will perform this." Isaiah 9:7 (KJV)

CONTENTS

Introduction

Until the last decade of the twentieth century it was a rare thing to find a book written on spiritual warfare about cities and nations. Around the late 1980's there began a flood of these books onto the market. At first they were controversial but interestingly, many became bestsellers. The books were instrumental in God's hand for awakening Christ's body to the work of intercession for cities and nations. Many of us read the books and God strengthened our calls to intercession. I was one of those. This book tells part of an unfinished story — of that call to intercession — for Beijing, China.

When the Lord called me to write this book at the end of 1994, He spoke firstly from Joshua 4:3. Here the Israelites, who had just crossed the river Jordan, were told to take up twelve stones from its middle, one for each of the twelve tribes. It was important that the children of Israel make a memorial so that future generations who had not experienced the power of God could understand and fear the Lord.

As I considered this scripture, I knew the revelations of God, the lessons learnt and the love of God we had felt during our intense season of prayer for the city of Beijing were not just for me to enjoy but for others who would follow as well.

A short while after the writing had begun, the Lord spoke a second time from Esther 3:2. This verse recorded Mordecai's reaction to the king's command to bow to Haman. Just as Mordecai did not give in to the pressure to bow down to this Haman (who was later exposed as a destroyer of the Jewish people), so the Lord made it very clear that I was not to give in to the pressure that would come. As Mordecai was later to challenge Esther, so in like manner I was summoned to stand and obey the call of my Lord to continue the writing assignment. Mordecai said:

> *"For if thou altogether holdest thy peace at this time, then shall there enlargement and deliverance arise to the Jews from another place; but thou and thy father's house shall be destroyed: and who knoweth whether thou art come to the kingdom for such a time as this?"* Esther 4:14 (KJV)

Esther's call was to risk her life for the sake of her fellow Israelites. (God is never caught unawares and has always prepared a person He can use in crisis.) Esther was reminded that her only place of safety was in obedience to this call, regardless of the danger she perceived. If she failed to follow the Lord's instructions she would lose her protection, and glory.

Similarly, one theme of this book is that we need to obey the call to intercede, to bless and stand for divine purposes in our cities. Let's face it, there's a price to pay for agreeing with God's purposes in our lives — and in our cities. Conversely, failure to obey will force God to choose another for the birthing of deliverance. The one who rejects the call will disappear from the scene, or in the words of Mordecai *"perish"*. Samuel the Old Testament prophet said, *"... To obey is better than sacrifice..."* 1 Samuel 15:22c (KJV).

The book unfolded as I obeyed — as did also the prayer strategy before it — the story reported in Part 1 of this book. One verse has come frequently to me during my time in Beijing,

> *"If you are willing and obedient you shall eat the good of the land,.."* (Isaiah 1:19 NKJV).

My discovery has been the patience of a loving Father Who knew my heart and poured out His grace when the pressure came, so enabling my obedience. I'm thankful too, that He has been writing the lessons on my heart. And I've enjoyed the good of the land. Where would I be without such a Father God?

The historical content of the book is necessary to show the importance of intercessors understanding the heart of their city. In this aspect of history I have included just a minimum of information to avoid losing the reader altogether. So much about Beijing itself is tied up in history, having as it does, such a long one. Ahead of time therefore I apologise to the Chinese people should they feel an incomplete historical picture has been painted.

I am asked about the numbers of people committing to Christ in the capital city. It's a good question and I wish I could give an indication by way of reliable statistics. In a city of 14 million with registered and unregistered churches no one really knows. It is true that a vast number of people are coming to the Lord every day in China — the last estimate I heard was 30,000 per day. Some of these would definitely come from Beijing. Remember though that there are revival hotspots in several parts of the country (specifically Henan and recently a powerful revival in Shandong). However the capital has historically been a difficult place for Kingdom expansion. This is true of other capitals as well as Beijing, China. It is clear that many foreign and Chinese Christians are being led by the Holy Spirit to pray for the city. I firmly believe that things we have hardly begun to believe possible will become part of Beijing's history because of God's great love for the people, their city and nation. This book has been written as a call to persevere in repentance and prayer. God will keep His promises.

Over and over again in the course of writing, it was clear that this work firstly belonged to the Lord for His purposes, not for man's. The Holy Spirit *breathed* it into my being. There have been times when the instructions He gave were not easy to understand, and the reasons did not unfold until later — sometimes much later. These were times when He taught me principles and ways of doing things and it was in the *doing of them* that I learnt His ways. The humiliation is not always being able to give a satisfactory answer to those around me. There is also embarrassment in learning the theory *after* having done the practicum. I've learnt this is often God's way — rather than doing the theory first and then the practical lesson. The process of recording the prayer strategy story has involved therefore, a huge learning curve. Though there have been lots of times I wanted to give up, it has been the memories of all the times God has spoken and the unusual things He has done that kept me going!

This book was born in God's heart first and with this knowledge came the certainty that as God's project, it would succeed. I read somewhere that '*The past really happened, but history is what someone recorded.*' A prayer strategy that really happened, along with God's answers were something He wanted written down. Step by step, then, along-the-way entries of testimonies have been confirmed by the Holy Spirit as things He wanted added. This happened frequently in remarkable ways. It is thanks to my Heavenly Father that this work is now completed.

Unfortunately I can't mention here those who have invested time and energy for me and this project (during the prayer strategy and the writing of the book). However, the Holy Spirit knows who you are. He singles you out for blessing and I do too! ***Thank you!*** Your love and patience, editing helps, suggestions, encouragement, financial support and especially prayer will be rewarded with appropriate and extravagant blessing. This is the way I have prayed for you. May the Father richly bless each one of you.

Esther C. Stanley

PART ONE

CHAPTER 1

A Poor Wise Man

"There was a little city and a few men within it;
and there came a ***great king*** *against it and* ***besieged it****,*
and ***built bulwarks against*** *it. Now there was found in*
it ***a poor wise man*** *and he by his wisdom delivered*
the city; wisdom is better than strength...,
wisdom is better than weapons of war.."
Ecclesiastes 9:14,15,18a (KJV) (Emphasis added)

Deborah, Mary and Esther[1] sat in the living room of a famous professor in Beijing, the capital of China. On the wall stretching almost to the ceiling and nearly reaching the floor hung an ancient map of the city dating back to the seventeenth century. There were photos in abundance, a coffee table, a desk, a few chairs and lots of books. It was a relatively simple setting and there were no signs that this was where he had suffered years of humiliation by the Japanese.

No one would have guessed by his humble, courteous manner

[1] All names in this book have been changed so as to protect the identity of those involved. None of the names used hold association to anyone with the same name living in the city.

that he was a busy man. He had turned away television cameras yet made three appointments around the busiest weekend of the year to see three strangers. There could be no other reason than that the subject of the appointments was of great interest to him.

As he began he spoke with fervor and conviction. He told of days as a teenager when he would cycle through the streets just getting to know his city. He talked of features past and present, of geographical characteristics, of correct and incorrect records and of the city's origins. All three ladies could sense his joy as he told of days past when he spoke up for the city's preservation, when he spent hours preparing submissions for its development. Shining through all his discourse came a rare love for a majestically grand old city.

He spoke of a great problem. An inadequate water supply had been a weakness since the city's earliest days. Regardless of the population count, and no matter how much water was transported (even over long distances), there was never enough. This factor was still affecting major decisions about the capital's future. Perhaps only God knew how serious a problem it was in April, 1994.

The professor leaned forward until he was on the edge of his chair. With great enthusiasm evident in his broad smile he related a story close to his heart. From his youngest days he had been told Bible stories by his mother, who had passed away early in his childhood. There was one story that stood out above all the rest. He loved it so much that when he grew up he wrote a play about it. The story was of a poor wise man who delivered his city and nation. The story was about a general named Gideon.

About that time I had begun reading the story of Gideon afresh and was thinking of it in a new light. There was a way to pray for a city and I could hear teaching coming out of the pages. I had been asking the Lord what his plans were because by then I was aware of His guidance to pray for the city of Beijing. The story of Gideon came up *again,* unexpectedly, during this meeting with the professor and I took note. Amazingly, we had been given appointments with him at such a busy time, and afterwards I once more felt they had been a divine arrangement. It was the second week of April, 1994 and the idea of a prayer strategy had been in my mind for six weeks already. In February I had found myself reading a dry old history book entitled *"In Search of Old Peking"*.

Beginnings

I had been trying to avoid it among all the other books on the shelves until the day my hostess handed it over personally. It seemed that my intentions of finding something light to read weren't working, but I felt a strange urge to read this book.

The first couple of chapters were boring beyond description. An inner impulse compelled me to read on, so I flipped through the book to get some idea of why the Holy Spirit was drawing me to it. I read a few pages and another chapter and then finally the last pages, and I was hooked. It dawned on me — this book was historical yes, but not a truly chronological account and it was different from most history books. There was an ancient geographical history but it also documented facts which hinted at the spiritual history. It was a gold-mine of information of the city of Beijing, in English, and, if those inner promptings were anything to go by, it could help unlock history!

That sounds like a daring thing to say, but along with the knowledge I'd gained from this book, came a heightened awareness that I was responsible for what I did with the new knowledge. It was too late to back out now, to say I had never read it. This fresh information left me caught, informed and accountable to obey the

Revealer of secrets, the Holy Spirit. Of course He knew how much I had understood and 'caught on' to heaven's intention. Yes, there was an inkling that God had a plan on His mind.

Hearing from God:

There's nothing new under the sun, except in God's Son.
The One who's breathed life into these hearts, has called us apart,
To be one with His Son and history He has already begun.
The servant of the Lord should not strive,
But there are things He speaks to us that come alive.
Often a whispering, God's voice may begin like an inkling.
If you've set it free to God, yet it returns and again burns
— this idea is yours, formed and born of the Holy Spirit.
By Him it's affirmed.

Hearing from God and receiving His ideas is awesome, a gift,
But even more, an invitation to co-partnership with Him.
Firstly, though, this inspiration must pass some tests:
Does it increase the anointing of the Holy Spirit and leave you with rest?
Does it release God's will and purposes
and does it align with principles in His Word?
If so, this inspiration will "flow";
It will be easy to go with, how it creates a life of its own.
Then, to go with the flow and not stem it
Is a choice to be willing and not hem God in.

I had heard from God before, of course. In the process of coming to China there had been a dream telling me not to go directly to the mainland, as others I knew had, but rather to go first to Taiwan. This was the door that in time, opened, and I knew to go through when it was presented. Again, on a short visit to the capital in the lead-up to living in China there was a very real visitation from Heaven as I walked across Tiananmen Square. Suddenly, my attention taken off the surroundings and as though in another world, verses 6 and 7 from Psalm 121 became the focus of my hearing.

> *"The Lord will keep you from all evil: he will keep your life. The LORD will keep your going out and your coming in from this time forth and even for ever more"* (AMP).

These verses had come up consistently enough during my journey with God to be dubbed one of my "life scriptures". On the other hand, the peace I was left with and the location where it happened were significant and I believed God was calling me to serve Him in this city. This was later confirmed and the call grew stronger with prayer. There were other times and ways God had spoken but mostly about my own or the lives of others. Now He was talking of things on a huge scale and that was very different.

The Plan

Discovering the plan God had on His mind was quite overwhelming. I had read and studied John Dawson's book, *Taking our Cities for God*,[2] before leaving my home country in August 1992. I also recalled spiritual battles previously encountered and recog-

[2] John Dawson, *Taking our Cities for God,* (Creation House, 1982).

nized them now as being strategic-level intercession. Just a year and a half later the thoughts were quickly coming together and I began asking myself serious questions. How does one take on a city? To know where to start was a headache in itself. Even going places in Beijing can take hours, and it was quickly obvious that without a strategy one could spend a life-time and get nowhere. I had few ideas of how to begin but consciously determined willingness to co-operate with God. I wondered how the necessary help would come to this city of all places.

A week later I became bold and told my good friends Abraham and Sarah. They had just come back from a conference on spiritual warfare. I wondered if anybody would really understand, but only the week after that, they introduced me to Mary. A first-time visitor just arrived in Beijing Mary had a heart for spiritual mapping. It was as simple as that. Mary was of Chinese lineage and associated with the spiritual warfare conference hosts. Here was someone who had received a little more learning in this field than I! We were being led to work together. The information assembled began to dovetail with startling clarity. In the research, discussions and prayer we felt united in the conviction that God was unveiling key city secrets of bygone days.

Grappling with the whole idea of a prayer strategy for Beijing included facing some formidible challenges. As resident guests of the Chinese we wanted to respect and abide by their laws. Regardless of precautions anybody could see that carrying out a prayer project in this city wouldn't be without risk.

It was challenging, though, to think of many gone before who had yielded tears, intercession and even given their lives to share the good news about Jesus. I began to think about the prayer warriors and great heroes of the faith who had doubtless spent hours in prayer for this great capital. I wondered if others had prayed about or "caught wind" of the secrets of the city for strategic prayer.

In this huge metropolis with a few small English libraries and no safe communication links with the outside world, asking how we could find such people seemed futile.

Secrets of the City

What are the secrets of a city? They aren't really private but God's enemy has made secret those dark things which have kept the city in bondage. (People without God love evil rather than right ways. They unknowingly believe and co-operate with the lies of their father the devil, inadvertendly permitting and welcoming the cover of darkness.) We felt the Holy Spirit and the Word of God were exposing the enemy's hidden secrets to help us be more effective in prayer.

In Chapter 2, we will look at some of these facts about the city which were then uncovered for us, but meanwhile we will continue to follow the pathway of God's leading for the prayer strategy. We have talked about hearing the Father's plan of prayer. How did we know it was His will? Would it increase the anointing and life of the Holy Spirit? Would it release God's will for us and the city? Did it line up with the principles in the Word of God?

The prayer strategy — God's will?

Perhaps others had been given prime keys through research and prayer to unlock the spiritual history of Beijing. We did interpret as significant though, the constant release of information about the city and revelation coming from God. There were lots of handicaps to manage: language barriers, "black holes" of history, records both accurate and inaccurate, inaccessible libraries and personal time pressures, yet a flow of relevant data kept coming. In the most unlikely surroundings the Lord appeared to be making it easy for us to proceed with our research. I can only describe it as a river and we were being carried in the flow of its current. After more prayer we stepped out.

Stepping out:

To follow God — now that's risky,
but faith is taking a possibility, the evidence of hope unseen.
If you've heard a word or even *think* you've heard from God,
There's always the chance it's not God and you've got it wrong.
However, the only way to really know
Is to step out and ask Him to show you.
And trust, of course, can only grow until it's a way of life, not a last resort.
The key to following God is to love Him;
If you're in love, it's easy to obey
But it nonetheless requires the exercising of faith,
And that's the simple way to avoid sin.
In every phase of the Christian life we must step out in God's grace
On what we hear from Him.
Going forward step by step is to find the way
Providence has prepared for us and when we trust and obey
He grants us more of His revelation.

In stepping out Mary and I shared the burden God had laid on our hearts with a few friends. The timing of our appointments with the professor fell just before the first group meeting in the second week of April. The favor we received from the professor, his unusual love for the story of Gideon and his committed interest in the city's origins and its future were clear signals God had prepared the way. Good connections had been made; it was not difficult to believe God's will was falling into place, and we were part of it. As I prepared to share the strategy from Gideon's battle with our friends, I found affirmation from Mary, who had been given similar guidelines from the Lord, during her study of this Bible warrior.

The Prayer Strategy — linked with principles of God's Word?

Before sharing the strategy I want to mention how uniquely God spoke to us from Judges 6 to 8. Our instructions often paralleled or bore extreme similarity to the Gideon story. It is one of the Bible's most unusual battles. However, of all the verses in Judges which speak about Gideon, only six in Chapter 7 specifically mention what happened in the first ambush. In contrast to this 58 verses were given to:

- Gideon's Preparation
- The army's preparation
- Their positioning for battle

- **Gideon's Preparation**

He was hiding in an out-of-the-way winepress, when God called him "mighty man of valour", or "man of fearless courage". Gideon asked a lot of why questions and then started with excuses. "I'm the poorest" and "I'm the youngest in my father's house" amounted to telling the Lord "I think you should choose somebody with money to lead an army and you're doing this in the wrong way. You should select the oldest, someone with more experience in the field and more likely to be a leadership candidate, rather than the youngest." The Lord answered both the questions and excuses with much the same wording.

> *"Go in this your might and you shall save Israel from the hand of Midian. Have not I sent you?" (6:14, AMP)* and *"Surely I shall be with you and you shall smite the Midianites as one man" (6:16, AMP)*.

The Lord wanted Gideon to be *certain* this command was coming from Heaven and that His presence would go with him.

By the way he asked questions at the beginning we know Gideon did NOT choose this assignment! Instead, consider skid marks up and down the bare ground beside the winepress! The Bible records his readying process in detail; especially his requests for confirmation and signs. God graciously granted them. Gideon's response is understandable knowing the odds stacked against him and the huge ramifications of his actions — either total victory or total defeat. In fact, in my mind, the story contrasts the powerful, numerically strong and supposedly invincible army of the enemy with the weak, outnumbered, inexperienced Israelite leader and his gang of 300.

We gasp with bated breath as God "does it all wrong"! The Bible narrative makes it clear though that neither the choice of leader nor the unheard-of strategy was any accident. In fact, it was an impossible situation for the Israelite camp to win without God. I believe it was intended that Gideon would only be seen as the fallible human he really was, for victors and vanquished alike were to see the glory of this battle as belonging to the victorious Creator, Warrior, Almighty God.

I suggest that God chose Gideon *because* he was not an experienced warrior. This captain wasn't skilled. He simply asked questions and asked for signs. He trusted what he heard and obeyed. To trust and obey is the wisest way to go on!

My Preparations for Leadership

While ascertaining exactly who God wanted to lead the prayer strategy for Beijing, I easily put myself in Gideon's shoes and had similar excuses to offer! Of all the people among my acquaintances, I was the youngest in terms of time lived in China. As well, to lead a team with very little leadership experience into an operation that I had never thought much about or even seen attempted was a little crazy! This story would not have happened without divine interaction.

I felt I understood Gideon's predicament — being surrounded by an enemy with a savage conquering ambition, then being asked by God to become a general and go to war. In fact I could see a lot of parallels between Gideon's pre-battle siege conditions and my preparations in Beijing to engage in strategic spiritual warfare.

From its earliest origins the Beijing area was a powerful and independent state. For over ten centuries it was a strategic trading and military post, often the site of power struggles and rebellious uprisings. In 1215 AD the world's most ambitious and savage conqueror, Ghengis Khan, made blazing history when he burned down the City of Swallows (or Chengdu[3] , the central capital of the then reigning Qin dynasty, approx. 20 kilometres southwest of modern day Beijing). His grandson Kublai Khan shifted the Mongol capital to Beijing, made it the centre of his entire empire and surrounded it with fortifications and bulwarks. The foundations of that capital are those of present-day central Beijing.

In the midst of research I recalled a verse of scripture. During my study of John Dawson's book, *Taking our Cities for God,* it had leapt off the page into my heart.

> *'There was a little city and a few men within it; and there came a* ***great king against it*** *and* ***besieged it****, and* ***built***

---

[3] This name Chengdu is not to be confused with the better-known modern gateway to the west, the Capital of Sichuan, also named Chengdu.

> ***great bulwarks against*** *it. Now there was found in it a poor wise man, and he by his wisdom delivered the city;.... Wisdom is better than strength...; Wisdom is better than weapons of war...."* Ecclesiastes 9:14,15a,16a,18a (KJV) [Emphasis added].

This passage mentions a great king besieging a little city, building fortifications and bulwarks against it. It sounded very similar to a past era in Beijing's history. These verses were clearly relevant to the Lord's mission of prayer for Beijing. He *had* earlier planted something in my heart, expecting this day of germination to come, *hadn't* He?

This seemed true, but like Gideon, I wanted another sign of His confirmation. (Why didn't I just trust and obey? I wondered if the Lord was tired of my grilling yet!) Considering what Heaven could be saying I thought a sure way to know if the Lord wanted me to go further than just researching the city would be if He gave us a prayer strategy. Having asked Him the question, I soon found myself engrossed again in the story of Gideon.

Gideon's Strategy — The Prayer Strategy

The first thing that struck me about the battle was how succinctly Gideon executed the ambush on the enemy's camp in *one* day. At the start of the middle watch during early morning hours Gideon and his company physically surrounded the enemy's camp, blew the trumpets, shouted the battle cry, *'A sword for the Lord and for Gideon!'* and entered the camp. The Lord set every Midianite's sword against his fellow and all the army fled (Judges 7:22). (Later Gideon called for reinforcements and together they chased after the kings, killed them and possessed the land entirely). That first ambush when all their enemies fled happened in one day. I'll call it 'The Gideon Day'.

When I first received 'The Gideon Day' strategy, it was like an open vision that stayed day after day. It was a picture of prayer teams visiting city streets all at once, concluding the same day. I had the sense our first "ambush" would be done cleanly, concisely and quickly. In the interest of safety and in respect of strict Chinese laws I could see God's wisdom in this strategy. I asked the Lord when He would like that one day to be.

In China every school year is divided into two semesters, from September 1st to early/mid January and March 1st to early/mid July. Since many of the foreign personnel with whom I was acquainted were involved in education, most would depart the city for their well-earned holiday at year's end in July. I knew that to maintain any sort of continuity with people in such a strategy, we had to complete all the research and conduct our day of prayer before the end of the current term. After my question to God, I felt June 12 was to be 'The Gideon Day'. I then thumbed back to Judges for the next instructions about the army.

• **Preparation of the Army**

Firstly, I noticed the Lord chose troops for Gideon's army. Many thousands responded to the call of duty when Gideon first blew the trumpet to prepare for war. When the Lord told Gideon to send all the troops home who were afraid or fainthearted it was an indication they were not called to battle. 'Should' and 'duty' didn't qualify. It was those who wanted to fight, who were willing and obedient to the heart's call that God was looking for. They were ones who knew the Author of the call, who found reflected in Him a love that casts out all fear.

Secondly, I noted that the Lord purposely reduced the army's personnel. If there were too many troops, the people would boast of the victory themselves instead of giving God the glory. I saw God was looking for humility rather than numerical strength, an army entirely dependent on Him. Wisdom is better than strength.

Thirdly, I observed God's final test for the army. The men were taken down to the brook and told to drink. There must have been a tense atmosphere since their enemies were not far away (Judges 7:7,8b). The men who passed this screening scooped water to drink with one hand but held weapons with the other; they were alert and ready for battle. In the midst of the seige (there were Philistines all around), their hearts were confident; they were diligent, mature and strong in the Lord and His love, potent in His power. Wisdom is better than weapons of war.

Finally, Gideon's army was down to three hundred. It was a good size for God but a foolish size for men. The odds against them were so great it would have been suicide to fight against their enemies in a conventional way. Presumably this was God's point, for the battle would not be won by might or power but by obedience to the Spirit of the Lord. Their preparations in many ways were spiritual and the Biblical records we are given indicate this battle was won in the spiritual realm first. As Gideon obeyed the Spirit of God, wisdom and supernatural energy were given him equal to the task. Gideon was a general by God's appointment.

Knowing these qualifications for Gideon's army wasn't much help to me though! I knew enough to look for mature Christian people in love with God, confident and unafraid, who wanted to pray for the city. At that point I had been living in the capital for just six months and knew only a few people. The Lord would have to choose this army just as He had appointed Gideon's army. After prayer, real peace entered my heart. It helped the decision-making process and with a handful of names I began to approach people.

The proposition was always the same. "Seek the Lord for a week. If you hear specifically from Him about your personal involvement as a leader (and later, as a team member) of the prayer strategy, then

I can accept your participation." At this juncture I wondered if the day of my reckoning had come. Who did I think I was anyway, asking people to come join a prayer strategy for the city, no less? The time had come to step forward and test the waters. Surely some really felt called to pray for the city and would hear from Heaven if this was of Him.

It was affirming that of the people who said they had heard a positive answer, four were on the committee of the Beijing International Christian Fellowship. One more committee member later became involved, although in the capacity of assistant leader. That was a total of five. (The laws of the land do not permit the position of full-time pastor to be filled or any foreigner seeking pastoral work to be permitted a visa. All positions of responsibility in the church in Beijing and in other such fellowships then and at the time of writing are voluntary.) In those days personnel on the committee numbered seven. Think of it! Five out of seven members of the church's governing body had apparently heard specifically from the Lord about their involvement and in so doing had indicated agreement. I felt this must be the Lord's doing.

We finally gathered together on April 17. At that first meeting Mary and Esther, Abraham and Sarah, Deborah, Miriam, Joshua and Timothy gathered and began to lift a canopy of praise. There was a list of things to do. After praise and worship we were to wait on the Lord for His word to come through any spoken prophecies. Then I would share teaching about Gideon and his army's preparation. Mary had done a great job in researching. Now her return home was imminent and we wanted to pray and bless her. Following that there would be prayer which turned out to be a commissioning of the prayer strategy leader.

We will now look at one more lesson from Gideon's life. How was Gideon taken from the call and commissioning — to the final positioning for battle?

- **Positioning for the Battle**

God called Gideon, then responded to his hesitant steps forward in answer to the call. It was a most unlikely start for God's man of the hour. We have talked in detail about his why questions and reasonings about how things were the way they were. The nation was in defeat. People were living in fear, hunger and poverty and were under siege. It was an hour of desperation. Gideon was not the most confident man in town, a point we learnt at the beginning of the story when he was found hiding.

Then came the dialogue with the angel of the Lord (whom at first glance may have seemed a weary traveller unaware of current news). The cramped conditions, the strange way of threshing grain at night, the deathly silence of it all and the panic and dread of everyday life was out in the open. The angel of the Lord started, *"The Lord is with you...."* (Judges 6:12, AMP). Gideon asked that if this was true, then *why* had all this befallen Israel? *Where* were the signs of divine favour? Or did the wonderful things grandparents had told their grandchildren about getting out of Egypt, stop then? Gideon was probably more ignorant about the disobedience issues than the elders of the nation were, but he still believed that God's presence meant victory. He acknowledged there wasn't a single person — except the Lord God Almighty — who could get them out of the siege alive and free.

He still had *faith*, and *had* responded to the angel with a cry for help. I doubt that Gideon was as interested in the nation's welfare as he was in his own, but while hiding underground near no-man's-land the angel of the Lord appeared. The call pronounced Heaven's name for him — *"a mighty warrior"* — and announced his commissioning — *"Have not I sent you?"* Now from Gideon, commitment was required. It was formed at this time of crisis, through the angel's confrontation, in pain that was keenly personal.

At last the Almighty had a man he could work with, somebody

who would listen. Perhaps for his own reasons, he would nevertheless fulfill heaven's purpose. Gideon had cried out for a personal need (his life), but God needed a deliverer who would listen to His instructions. When Gideon's heart was ready for commitment, God's purpose and Gideon's need fell together in one accord. The Lord fulfilled both as He began to use Gideon.

The call on Gideon's life now meant his own future was unavoidably tied up with the nation's. Question by question and step by step, he grew stronger. Point by point, the preparation of the army and the positioning for battle was determined. It was two-way communication God and Gideon had going, based on commitment. God can use anybody who is committed to Him, even an imperfect vessel like a young man hiding for his life.

My first six months in China climaxed with a period of crying out to God for personal revival. The tears came naturally but the fire of God burned and worked change in a unique way. In the time of pain the commitment was made and forgotten, almost. Then, in the crisis of spiritual drought, this was the only answer I could give to the all-surpassing One. It was also a dangerous thing to say, but I had promised the Lord that I would do anything He asked. God had heard. He had intertwined His purposeful commitment with mine. For years I wondered why He had chosen me, until the day He indicated how to finish this chapter. He reminded me of that promise of commitment.

The Commissioning

As foolish and weak as I now felt, I knew the bottom line had to be saying yes to God. The rest would have to be left up to Him. The prayer group team leaders gathered round for the commissioning prayer. The final word I had for the day was given, "Yes"! Then a prophecy came about being used to help with other prayer strategies in the future. I felt that this word was confirmation of the

Lord's will for me, at least to lead this prayer strategy in Beijing. Another prophetic word I had been given less than two months before came to mind. It spoke of being used mightily by the Lord, *"You're right on time in God's schedule and you're in position ...."* The word made a lot more sense to me now than when I had first heard it. I believed at last that God had posted me to this appointment for His strategic purposes.

The grace and peace encountered during our times together in the prayer strategy and which I experienced personally was something I will never forget. There was a powerful consciousness of God's love and it staggered me that the Creator of the Universe was being so intimate. There was nothing I could point to for all this except that He loved our obedience. The subject of our prayer — revival for the city of Beijing — must have been a purpose very dear to His heart. Confidence grew inside me and I felt God would be faithful to complete what He had begun.

The story of what God had begun is Part 1 of this book, a prayer project carried out between April and July 1994. There were six group meetings incorporating times of identificational repentance and prayer visits to the seven altars in Beijing. Thc map from the book *In Search of Old Peking* described the shape of a demon god built into the layout of the central city plans. Chapters 2 to 5 of this book detail the preparatory steps we took to pray at the city sites designated parts of that god. On June 11 we prayed indoors the entire day and on June 12 we prayed on the streets. There were eight team leaders and 38 team participants, while a few out-of-town visitors brought the total to 40.

Walking through the story I'll share biblical principles of prayer warfare that can be applied to other cities. You'll get a taste of China, and at the end of each chapter I'll list prayer points. The anointing of the Father's love was perpetuated through the months I lead the strategy; however, the love God showed was not for me alone. He wanted, and still wants us to pray that the people of Beijing and China would know His deep, unfathomable, unconditional love. So much love!

Father, in Jesus' name I ask that You would pour out Your Spirit on the readers of this book. Thank you for the privilege of sharing this story with them. I pray they would know Your love for them and that they would be moved today to give it away to someone who is lost. I pray You'll be able to say to each one that day before the judgment throne, "Well done!" May they be one with You just as the Father and Son are one in everything they do. May we be one in Your love that the world will know whom You have sent. I ask these things by the power of Your Spirit for Your sake and the extension of Your Kingdom.

In Jesus' name, Amen.

CHAPTER TWO

Where Did We Begin (to Strike Down The Enemies)?

"The LORD said to him, "But I will be with you, and you shall ***strike down*** *the Midianites,* ***every one*** *of them."* Judges 6:16 (NRSV) (Emphasis mine)

When the Lord called Gideon he was hailed a "mighty warrior" who would deliver Israel and strike down every enemy. The mission was a battle. In a similar way, the prophetic words which the Lord gave us in the first group meeting of the prayer strategy indicated His work as a stubborn warrior and our role in His army.

> *"You have not seen stubbornness until you have seen My stubbornness. Move only as you are carried in My Spirit. It is for My Name's sake that I will do this great work."*

We interpreted this word as a reminder of the holy, immovable character of the Lord whose power is stronger than the most stubborn enemy. Just as Gideon only acted according to God's instructions, we were charged to do likewise. A second word from the Lord came:

> *"I saw a picture of two armies. One was the Terra-cotta soldiers of ancient Xian — the most famous army in the country [of China]. The world knows they were a mighty army. The other army is one being raised up by the Lord [in Beijing] — and it is such as has not been seen in the country, ever. It will be a beautiful army arrayed with the garments of the Lord, covered with His anointing. This is His authority and as He sends His army they will be protected and victorious because of Who is sending them. They will be covered with that which is like the dew of Mount Hermon [like the precious oil] which ran down Aaron's beard and they will stand invincible because of God's authority."*

We viewed this vision as referring to the prayer soldiers who would intercede for Beijing in 1994. The reference to Mount Hermon with dew on it is from Psalm 133 and was likened to the precious anointing oil which ran down Aaron's head and beard. Oil was used to anoint the priests and as it ran down from the head and beard it consecrated the whole body. This picture spoke to us of the way the Holy Spirit would anoint, protect and bring unity to all of us. It was a most wonderful thing promised us!

I knew that unity is an essential ingredient for a prayer initiative, that a spirit of unity could only come from all of us following Jesus Who is our Head. It meant taking up our priestly role of intercession and being led by the Spirit of God before we could receive the promise of Psalm 133. Unity therefore had to be a gift from Heaven and the reward of keeping it would be God's fullest blessing. This was all true, yet it wasn't anything we could "do". In fact as things progressed there was a lot that God seemed to be doing and not very much that I could do. Perhaps it didn't appear so, but I felt helpless most of the time!! Feelings of awkwardness were replaced with grateful thanks as Father answered cries for help. My main job was reaching up to Him to get the next step.

What was on God's heart for our city? What is His purpose for any of us in the city where we live, where He has called us? Jeremiah 29:7 tells us:

> *"But seek the welfare of the city where I have sent you into exile, and pray to the Lord on its behalf, for in its welfare you will find your welfare"* (NRSV).

Paramount to receiving blessing in the capital was our praying for the city and seeking its well-being and prosperity. Psalm 122 is a song along similar lines for the city of Jerusalem, uttered for the favour of relatives and friends and the house of the Lord. We too, need to seek the city's blessing for the same reasons — for individuals, family, and the expansion of the Kingdom of God according to God's call. We are personally involved.

When I went to Bible School we learnt that Abraham was blessed to be a blessing. He received rich abundance from His Father God and then was called to dispense that good to others, including the nations of the world. As heirs of God's family we share individually and corporately in the abundance and increase of favour as Abraham did. Likewise, we are also blessed to pass it on — to give the Father's blessing to the nations.

This is a huge call, and I would ask what it means to be a blessing. In China even the Buddhists believe that religion should include learning to be kind, dispensing good, showing love to others. We as Christians do these things neither to earn merit points nor to earn the Father's love (our motivations are different), yet from scripture we see that kindness, goodness and love are aspects of God's character. Certainly, our lives must reflect the Father's nature to the world around us. The question is: Whose blessing do we share, ours or the Almighty's? Another way to put it would be the now well-known motto, "receiving God's love and giving it away." We first need to "be" God's children, then give away His love.

What is the Father's ultimate purpose for blessing the nations? The promise was that all the families of the earth would receive and know the Father's love (His fullest blessing). When the promise was first given to Jacob it was guaranteed to his Offspring (singular, not plural) which is a reference to Christ. For those who received Christ Jesus, the promise given to Abraham, Isaac and Jacob would also come; it was for all the families of the earth. The Father's desire has always been that none would miss out on joining His family or from the inherited blessings that come to those in His family. Psalm 72:17 says,

> *"His name shall endure for ever; His name shall be continued as long as the sun...And men shall be blessed and bless themselves by Him; all nations shall call Him blessed!"* (AMP)

We aren't there by a long way! It *is* the promise given us by God, of what He will do among all the nations of the earth. It's the Father's love in us and praying His heart that will take us there.

Moses went a huge step forward in prayer on this subject of blessing the nations. He *required* the presence of the Lord on Israel, *otherwise the surrounding nations would not see the blessing of God on them.* If the nations were to want the blessing of God, they had to first see the result on Israel — how it outweighed the abundance, goodness, favour and love from any other source. Listen to the way Moses talked to God!

> *"And Moses said to the Lord, If Your presence does not go with me, do not carry us up from here! For by what shall it be known that I, and Your people have found favor in Your sight? Is it not in Your going with us so that we are distinguished, I and Your people, from all the other people upon the face of the earth?"* Exodus 33: 15,16 (AMP)

This was a self-less prayer *for the sake of the nation and God's purpose for the surrounding countries.* The key to Moses' prayer is understanding that without His presence, God's favour is absent. Putting it the other way around, the absence of God's favour — His presence is not there — is literally a curse, and it is clear why Moses was desperate. The next question we need to ask in praying for God's blessing on a city is, What keeps His presence from increasing in the city and nation?

That there are enemies to God's presence in the city would be a point we all agree on. Where though, did we begin to strike down the enemies of God's presence? (At last I have got to the point of this chapter!) The answer was another question: In what ways had the people sinned? We had to know exactly to repent specifically. That would help us to know the curses the people might be under. In His call to Jeremiah God was very clear about *how* he was to proceed. The first step began with rooting out.

Only the year before, in 1993, a kind friend had taken time to tell me one of her recent revelations. It was about Jeremiah 1:10:

> *"See, I have this day appointed you to the oversight of the nations and of the kingdoms, to root out and pull down, to destroy and to overthrow, to build and to plant"* (AMP).

This verse was all about the authority established, decreed and given her, as she sensed God's call to intercede for the land around her. A series of historic stories and information suddenly popped up soon after this and she was able to pray more specifically using her authority from Heaven. It was in a remote part of mid-west China and the Holy Spirit had taught her sequentially how to root out, then to pull down, destroy and overthrow. It's funny but the story had stuck fast to me, like a girdle about my waist. Truthfully, Father had used a simple memory to encourage me. Now it was our turn to do some rooting out, or digging up.

Spiritual Mapping

It was not difficult to understand that we needed to do some research. 'It must be a matter of first things first', I thought; 'If there is a problem, there must be a root, or a cause'. In those days I didn't know the term spiritual mapping, having only just heard it from Mary!

Spiritual mapping is rooting out physical signposts of the past that betray spiritual concerns to pray about. A good part of spiritual mapping is research or study, yet I have found the Holy Spirit always very instrumental in this process. The result of following His leading has exposed physical places where satan has established historical strongholds of darkness. These strongholds are intended to keep the people from receiving the gospel of Jesus Christ.

When the Lord gave me the assignment of researching the city of Beijing, He came in His nature as the Revealer of Secrets. I grew up in a Christian home and from a child believed that He knows everything about everybody and everything about history.

> *"He reveals deep and secret things; He knows what is in the darkness, and light dwells with Him"* (Daniel 2:22, NKJV).

His presence goes with us when as His agents, we bring the deep and secret things to the light. Fear cloaks hidden things but in bringing them to the light of truth, they are unmasked and disarmed; fear and deception are broken. This is an important job! To intercede in the gaps we must know where the spiritual breaches in the city walls are.

Our Spiritual Mapping for Beijing

In Chapter 1 we learnt that the nephew of Ghengis Khan, Kublai Khan built a new capital for the Mongal empire in 1215AD. Called Dadu, it's location was 20 kilometers north-north-east of the City of Swallows, or Chengdu which was burnt to the ground by the Mongolian army. The present day capital city of Beijing mirrors the old Mongolian capital, particularly the central city location and layout. (See Appendix D, The Walls and Gates of Old Beijing). A rather famous city, Beijing was the capital of the country with the world's largest population for all of the 20th Century. Here in 1911 the last of a long line of emperors abdicated. The child emperor, Pu Yi, opened up the emperors' palace which had been forbidden to the commoner for centuries. Located in the center of the capital city, it still holds considerable importance. In English it is called the 'Forbidden City'. There China was declared a nation under communism on October 1st, 1949. Again on October 1st, 1966 the central city became the birthplace of the Cultural Revolution which sent many people to their early deaths. On June 4, 1989 this heart of the city again became the center of the world's attention and people still talk (and avoid talking) about the events which took place. So much death had occurred in other centuries here, as well as in the horrific events of the late 20th century, but why so much ado in the central city?

To submit one answer, I would like to briefly compare two maps of the earliest city plans. We will discover that two foundational maps of the present city though separated by two centuries and a war, are very similar. We will learn how the physical signposts of the past revealed spiritual issues for prayer. First we will look at plans for the city completed in 1264AD by Kublai Khan.

Kublai Khan's City Plan

Construction began on Kublai Khan's city, Dadu, in 1215. He was a Mongolian emperor, not Han Chinese. Perhaps that was a good enough reason that the city plans were a little different from the 'norm'. Plans for ancient cities in China usually had four sides and three gates on each side, a total of twelve gates in the outer city wall. Inside the city extending from the twelve gates were straight roads which ran parallel to and crossed each other forming a grid, chessboard effect.[1] This meant ancient cities were almost square. Cheng-du, or the City of Swallows, the Qin dynasty city which Kublai Khan burnt to the ground, had met these requirements perfectly. In Dadu however, there were only *two* gates on the north side and three gates on each of the other three sides of the city walls. Dadu was not square and had only 11 gates, a significant deviation. (See Appendix D). We'll look at the reason Chinese records give for this difference when looking at the second city map, shortly.

We now go back to the Mongols whose reign under Kublai Khan and the Yuan dynasty lasted approximately 98 years (1271–1368). The foreign Mongolians were defeated by a revolutionary Chinese army in Dadu; the imperial palace was destroyed and much of the city was burnt to the ground in the war. The capital was moved south to Nanjing until nearly two centuries later when Yong Lo relocated his capital in Beijing. After a four year battle securing his

---

[1] The chessboard effect, or white against black, is symbolic of a belief called dualism. Basically this belief attributes good and evil with equal status, rather than good triumphing over evil in the manifest presence of the Almighty God and His son Jesus Christ. Though expression of this belief of dualism continues today by some, still in architecture, we must not bring judgment since many people are without the knowledge of God's Word and forgiveness of sins and have not been redeemed themselves — let alone their culture.

heir-apparent right to rule as emperor, he moved the capital from Nanjing back to the current location of Beijing. He spent 15 years (1405–1421AD) building a city he could be proud of. The city's name was changed from Beiping (northern peace) to Beijing (northern capital) on completion of the city's restoration.

Yong Lo's City Plan (1421)

Though I cannot quote a reference to say the plans were the same, Chinese historical specialists have claimed close links between the second city and first city plans, Yong Lo's city and Kublai Khan's city. There were several major aspects bearing uniformity, but we will mention just one. Again there were only two gates in the northern city wall, bringing the total number of gates to 11.

How did Yong Lo choose the plans of his city? The newly appointed military first-in-command, a former Buddhist monk and an astrologer, handed him a sealed package containing the plans. Depicted in them was the layout of a symbolic god. The capital was mapped and built after this figure.

Mary researched this creature and discovered he was a man of war with a spear in his right hand. Known as one of the Chinese deities, ne zha, the people called him a formidible warrior; he is depicted with knees bent as if ready to attack and seize his prey. In many legends he was pictured as stubborn and unbeatable.

Was there any significance to two cities being built almost the same? Three sources confirmed Yong Lo's city of 1421 as relating to the body of the eight armed god.[2] Whether the particular account attributed this figure with eight arms, or in others six arms and three heads, in any case the number of limbs totalled 11. This was the reason for Kublai Khan's deviation from the Chinese

---

[2] Zhang Zi Chen and Li Yue Nan, *Folklore of Beijing, 8 Arms Ne Zha City* (Shanghai Art and Literature Publishing House, June 1982) pp 1-5)

model of ancient cities, which "normally" had 12 gates. Dadu city had 11 gates in the outer city wall, each one representing a head, leg or arm.[3]

Wasn't this too long ago, you may ask? Is there any reason for us as intercessors to pray about these physical parallels the people made 7 centuries ago between city streets, gutters, gates, a bridge, lakes, walls and open spaces linking a superimposed Chinese warrior deity to the city's plans? The curse definitely needed to be broken over the land and the people, one place at a time. It seems from records given us that locally this legend has been kept "alive" since the Yuan Dynasty's Dadu, until the present time. In Beijing at the end of 1992, there was a conference marking the anniversary of the 720th year since the building of Dadu. A specialist in Yuan Dynasty history, Chen Gao Hua, is reported to have said that the 11 gates of the Yuan Dynasty, Dadu, were precisely those apportioned as gates according to the legend.[4] Apparently, in 1992, this was still important.

Why did the kings build their cities after this creature? Over and over the books told us the plans were based on what was reported as "very correct" principles of geomancy, a form of divination. By definition divination is a form of control, a superstitious way of trying to plot the course of future events, thereby causing them to happen. The Chinese form of geomancy is called Feng Shui, the use of controlled geographic plotting on a small or large scale to shape the future. The motivation to use divination is always for profit and false predictions abound. It would appear two kings who did not know any other way of defending their city chose to invoke beings in the spiritual world which were recommended to them to guard the city. As children of the Most High God we later

---

[3] Shi Lian Fang *Beijing Alleyways, Plane Names and Interesting Tales* (China International Broadcasting Publishing House, April 1992) p. 76

[4] Zhao Luo Zhu *Beijing Stories* (Chinese Tourism Publishing House ISBN 7-6032-0774-4) p.31

initiated repentance to the Lord for idolatry and divination (and prayed over the places involved), for this people had never known the Almighty God, (Who is the greatest Warrior and Lord of all), nor their need to repent. (Appendix D details.)

The truth about these city plans one day struck home. The same war-like buddhist god had twice been built into the central city plans of Beijing. (Firstly this was in 1215 in Dadu City, and secondly in 1421, in Yong Lo's City. This is also the location of the current city.) Now we could understand the city's great need for prayer in a new way! Was this one reason why there had been so much death?

Praying God's Plans

It was encouraging that the Lord had previously declared to us His stubborn and unbeatable nature, and now the fact that He knows history was emblazened to us in flashing lights. The counterfeit of God's salvation plan, reflecting stubbornness, hatred and rebellion appears very clearly in the original defense system of Beijing. Oh, how wonderful that we could claim the promise given in Isaiah 26:1:

> *"In that day shall this song be sung in the land of Judah; We have a strong city; salvation will God appoint for walls and bulwarks"* (KJV).

Now there was a strong motivation to pray — that the Lord would arrange the mightiest defense system of all — and that salvation would be set up as walls and bulwarks.

Just as in Bible days, the gates of Chinese cities were where day-to-day transactions occurred. Legal deeds, graduations and knighting of soldiers, marketing and news reporting were usual activities at these gates. On the huge rostrom above the gate called "Tiananmen" (literally, the Gate of heavenly peace and harmony, located at the northern end of the Square), the king would sit to bring pronouncement of the latest edicts of the empire. This was the site of the emperor's wedding and here he was crowned. Announcements concerning justice, the sentencing to death of prisoners and the pardoning of others was carried out. Those portals running in a straight line south to the Temple of Heaven were delegated part of the king's highway, and were kept specifically for the emperor to pass through. The gates were very important to the city, and every aspect of life could be found represented in one of them.

City gates provided a strategic place for the city's defense. Enemies would storm these gates and many bulwarks were built to avoid vulnerability, later even a moat was added. Fortresses were built there and within the gate area other buildings such as temples were constructed to incur the favour of, for example, the god of war.

The gates represent the vulnerable places of the city. Isaiah 62:10 speaks of the gates and we are commanded:

> *"Go through, go through the gates; prepare ye the way of the people; cast up, cast up the highway; gather out the stones: lift up a standard for the people"* (KJV).

Through the leading of His Holy Spirit, God wants us to lift up a standard against the enemy, to get rid of him and put him to flight (Is 59:19). Psalm 127:4 and 5 tells us:

> *"As arrows are in the hand of a mighty man; so are the children of the youth. Happy is the man that hath his quiver full of them: they shall not be ashamed, but they shall speak with the enemies in the gate"* (KJV).

In the middle column of the King James Version, *"shall speak"* is also equated to mean *"shall subdue, or destroy"*. Through the power of Jesus' name, the gates of hell (the places where satan has tried to take authority) will not prevail against those in the body of Christ, who have Jesus as their life's strong foundation and who use their God-given authority and jurisdiction.

The prayer strategy — a clearer dimension

The prayer strategy took on clarity and a new dimension. Our Gideon's Day would involve 8 teams going to all the places mapped as parts of the warrior-god's body to pray. That would be no small task. There were thirty-three places and there was lots of research work to do in the two and a half months before June 12. Only seven centuries of history! Thankfully, reading it all wasn't necessary! The research teams did have to identify and locate each of the designated places. Secondly, maps outlining the thirty-three localities were to be provided along with photographs, to facilitate easy location for prayer teams on our Gideon's Day. Thirdly, but definitely not in order of importance, team leaders were asked to record their spiritual impressions, burdens and words received from the Lord about each place. We wanted to do a thorough job in prayer while we were at it!

Breaking the arms of the strongman In that first group meeting, there was one more word form the Lord.

"Break the arms of the strongman."

This word kept coming back and was confirmed by others. What is a strongman? A strongman is somebody who guards a stronghold, a fortified place or castle. Right then the Lord was obviously speaking about a spiritual entity, as it would be uncharacteristic for Him to talk about breaking somebody's arms!

Shortly after I asked the Lord to show me exactly *how* to do this, I was involved in an accident. I sustained minor injuries only, so the group meeting was held as scheduled the next day. Our prayer for each other intensified. I do believe the incident was used by the Father to mould unity among us. There were signs that a spiritual battle had really begun. The situation resembled a minefield and we needed the next clue in the puzzle *before* we took the next step!

With more time on my hands while recouperating from the accident, I rested, and in a room on my own, too! Accommodation then meant sharing a dormitory room, and privacy was (and is often) rare. What a gift it was to stay at Abraham and Sarah's and have a place to pray out loud!

Puzzle Pieces — A vision of a dragon I had time to find one of the puzzle pieces on an audio-tape about intercession for China. An intercessor related a vision she had of a huge dragon which had four powerful feet. Trying to dislodge the dragon but finding herself weak and incapable, she called on fellow intercessors to help. She described how in the vision, each of the dragon's feet had a strong spirit attached to it and through these spirits of fear, rebellion, hatred and religion the dragon's control was perpetuated. In this way the people were gripped by the bloodthirsty dragon. As I pondered the account I remembered a similar vision I had had a few weeks earlier. It also left me feeling powerless, asking the Lord how to pray. How grateful I was to the Lord for this confirmation from the audio-tape!

Puzzle Pieces — Legends The Holy Spirit had clarified to us that the dragon had kept the people in bondage through a strong spirit of control. The Holy Spirit had also exposed the image of a warrior-god reflected in the city's plans. We were being led along the right trail because the Holy Spirit never lies. Some records repeatedly mentioned a few stories and gave much credence to them, so highlighting aspects which the Lord was exposing as strongholds of belief. The stories or legends themselves were not true to life but supported what the Holy Spirit was saying had kept the people bound. There was confirmation that divination (seen in the city plan) and control (by fear, hatred, rebellion through worship of the dragon, images of which are plentiful in China) were closely linked in historical belief systems.

Pieces dovetail We were not to deal immediately with these strongholds. At this time the Holy Spirit lead us in a pathway of humility, always a good rule of thumb when beginning any prayer strategy! Now, the urgency of the Lord's instructions to *"break the arms of the strongman"* became emphatic as I pondered the issues. According to the visions, one of the feet of the dragon was rebellion and hatred. Could these characteristics be superimposed on any geographical aspect of the city? Could this be the warrior-god posed with a spear? The Holy Spirit's direction grew poignant as I thought of the historical hatred of some Chinese towards foreigners. Understandably this was because of adverse treatment by foreigners over centuries from *many* nations. I then asked myself — 'How do you disarm rebellion and hatred?' And I answered: 'Through repentance and forgiveness.'

Now it was clear why we had had a few spiritual landmines blowing up around us. There were unsettled accounts left oustanding against foreigners, and our forefathers had been *part* of the problem. We had to deal with this sin before going on. Whew! What a relief to know what the next step would be! That step — repentance for the actions of our forefathers towards the Chinese — meant identifying with the sins of yesteryear, apologising to the Lord and asking for His forgiveness. (Called identificational repentance, this topic will be covered in Chapter Three.)

Repentance for the Sins of our Forefathers

At the third group meeting on May 8, 24 people gathered to repent. Although no special guests were invited, among us there were citizens of or those who could identify closely with, each of the 11 nations whose past actions towards China we repented of. Firstly we gathered in small groups according to national identity and reviewed offences committed against China. The historical record of sins made from research were read in each group after which a time of corporate repentance began. A representative from each nation stood to confess these sins before God and to an overseas Chinese who stood before us representing the Chinese people. We were grateful for this kind man, whose presence helped us be specific and real in our confessions. He then responded in prayer, forgiving and asking God to forgive and heal the nations represented.

As groups began to confess the sins of our forefathers it was a moving time. Part of our confession included admission of attitudes of superiority which we hadn't previously acknowledged and this up-front recognition of our sins in prayer to God and the Chinese was now done with real heart-brokenness. We recognized that the root sins of our forefathers still had a hold in *our* hearts, too. The nations we represented that day included Mongolia, Portugal, Italy, Holland, Britain, Russia, Japan, USA, Germany, France and Austria. Other nations we may have missed were covered in a general prayer at the end.

Confession of sin was not intended to be a statement justifying any nation's actions, rather it was contrition for the harm done and suffering inflicted on the Chinese. Some of the actions of colonial powers deeply humiliated the Chinese and have affected Sino-foreign affairs since the sixteeth century.[5] It is a sad fact that especially

[5] "*China's Black Eyes*", (Asia Week Magazine January 27, 1993) p.25

since the nineteenth century, missionary impetus has been considered 'western' and linked with the political expansionism of western colonial powers[6]. These sins included:

> intentional hostility and forceful takeover[7] ; sowing revenge and enforcing a slave mentality[8] ; not providing priests to teach Christianity as requested by Kublai Khan[9] ; trespassing on land; theft; inhumanity towards women and children; exploitation[10] ; sowing mistrust and fear; offences and disagreements within the body of Christ which led to the first emporal edict forbiding public teaching of Christianity in China[11]; disobeying laws as merchants and traders; forcing trade and concession of ports; introducing and enforcing drug addiction through the opium trade opening the doorway to a continuing problem today; forcing Chinese to relinquish land; forcing the concession of consulates and foreign embassies in Beijing[12] .

---

6 Hedda Morrison, *A Photographer in Old Beijing,* (Hong Kong, Oxford University Press, 1985, 1993)p. 6

7 Kublai Khan, nephew of Ghengis Khan, the leader of the largest empire the world has ever known, followed in the family tradition uncompromisingly securing supermacy over China in 1279. These were the first "barbarians" to conquer all of China, and the locals saw that the Mongolians had no right to do so, since they were foreigners and had acquired the territory by force. Madge Huntington, *A Traveller's Guide to Chinese History* (Henry Holt & Co., New York, USA, 1987) pp. 92,93

8 The local people hated Mongolian rule because set over them were Tartar and Moslem governors of foreign descent, each of whom treated the locals like slaves. Edited and with an Introduction by Milton Rugoff, *The Travels of Marco Polo* (New American Library of World Literature Inc., 1961) p. 138

9 Ibid., Kublai Khan asked for 100 priests to teach Christianity to his court, their purpose being to instruct the principles of Christian religion and to address the issue of whether idolatry and worship of evil spirits so strong in the east was correct, as well as to teach the seven arts. Kublai Khan said that if proof could be evidenced of the supremacy of Christianity, then he and all under him would become Christians. Two priests set out on the journey from Rome to Beijing but later turned back. The Emperor's invitation was never met.

10 When the Portuguese arrived in 1516 in Guangzhou, they sent an envoy with papers from

There were undoubtedly sins which we failed to confess, but we did take several hours to work through the list. There were a few countries whose national representatives yielded particularly memorable confessions. One of these was Mongolia. The Mongolians were the first foreigners to enforce their rule in China and when Ghengis Khan's hordes ransacked old Beijing, the burning, looting and raping continued unchecked for a month while many girls threw themselves from the city walls.[13] As Salome prayed, God gave her a picture of a soldier smashing a baby against a brick wall. This picture helped her to repent in sincerity and tears for the brutality and destruction which had been inflicted on the Chinese as a result of Mongolian rule.

When we came to Britain's confession it seemed to involve many of us — especially those of British ancestry. What a gift of repentance had been given Rebecca and Hannah, who asked God's forgiveness for hardness of heart, pride, forcefulness along with a desire to manipulate and control the Chinese for monetary profit! Then there came a real sense of being undone, of hearts breaking. At the end of this time there was a witness in our hearts that something had broken in the spiritual realm.

---

the King of Portugal to the Emperor of China. While awaiting a reply they robbed and looted Chinese vessels, kidnapped women and children and behaved with disrespect. Understandably, Chinese violence against the western presence was linked to this event, and hostility continued on both sides from then. Madge Huntington, *A Traveller's Guide to Chinese History* (Henry Holt & Co., New York, USA) pp 108-109.

11 Ibid., pp 114-115. The Jesuits, who arrived at the end of the sixteenth century tolerated the simultaneous practice of Bhuddist worship for Christian converts. The Dominicans and Franciscans later voiced disagreement with them on this and other things such as the proper term for God. The Vatican announced its support for the Dominicans and Franciscans but in 1720 the emperor Kang Xi was outraged by what he saw as "interference with his authority" and prohibited the further teaching of Christianity in China.

12 Ibid., pp 121-124. British imports of Chinese tea were six times more than its exports to China and to rectify this imbalance, the British encouraged the export of opium from India to China. In 1815 the Qing government officially banned the import of opium but the British offered bribes of silver coins and smuggled it in. A Chinese commissioner burned 20,000 chests of opium and the British declared war, which ended three years later with the signing of the Treaty of Nanking. Hong Kong was ceded to Britain, five trading ports were opened to British

Prayer and confession was amazingly specific. Some countries had more sins to deal with but everybody was doing their best to leave no sin unconfessed. We discovered that our willingness to repent was the need of the hour and that in all honesty we could not separate ourselves from the past. Considering the tremendous damage done to the nation of China, it was just a beginning and I believe more repentance is needed. However, as we prayed from our hearts in repentance, love for God and the Chinese people was very real that day in 1994.

After this we shared communion and everybody gave hearty assent as prayer was made to *"break the arms of the strongman"*. We began to praise the Lord and joy welled up in abundant worship. Then the Lord spoke to us:

> *"Where the glory of the dragon has rolled over the land, the glory of the Lord is now moving in wave upon wave over the land."*

Somebody began to laugh spontaneously and another word from the Lord came:

---

consulates and the Chinese paid a huge indemnity of one million silver dollars to the British. In 1844 similar treaties were made with the United States and France. In 1856 the second opium war broke out after further smuggling of opium and the arrest of a British captain charged with piracy. The Treaty of Tianjin in 1858 ceded more trading ports and benefits to westerners, made further allowances for the opium trade, allowed missionary activity and permitted foreign consulates in Beijing. There was reaction from the Chinese who found it hard to accept ratification of the treaty. This led to a foreign envoy being sent to the Qing Court and the Summer Palace in Beijing was burned down. Reconciliation through the 1860 signing of the Treaty of Beijing was short lived, but embassies were permitted in the capital. In 1899 Emperor Ci Xi planted ploys and encouraged a two month seige of foreigners, wanting foreigners out of Beijing. On the heels of the unrest the Boxer Rebellion was begun in 1900 by a secret Chinese order. The combined forces of Britain, Russia, Japan, USA, Germany, France, Italy and Austria were engaged in war, extending over the whole of North China. The last of the Unequal Treaties was then signed granting westerners a free hand for their trading and missionary interests and increased residential privileges while China paid 350 million US dollars in reparations.

[13] *The Forbidden City [China's Ancient and Modern Capital]* by Robert Farquhar and the Editors of the Newsweek Book Division (Published by Newsweek Book Division, 1972) p. 48

> *"Do not be afraid to laugh, 'for then were they filled with laughter, when the Lord released their captivity.'"* [Taken from Psalm 126:2 (KJV)]

A final prophetic word came to us from the Lord:

> *"'The Lord will sing over this city. He has wept for it. As the Lord loves Jerusalem and would have gathered it as a hen gathers its chickens under its wings, so the Lord would gather Beijing under His wings. The Lord has a plan of redemption for this city."*

After the meeting people expressed feelings of honor in their having participated. We'll probably never know until Heaven everything that was done that day. We had taken responsibility for our sin as we should have and this prayer was our duty. There was something wonderful about it all but it wasn't anything we did! The Father loves the Chinese so much that He had shared His love — tangibly. Somehow He had disclosed His emotions to our frail human hearts. Through this group of ordinary people, He had made His love work for the people of Beijing, not against them. In return we had glimpsed something profound and holy: the Almighty's heartbeat of love for Beijing.

PRAYER POINTS

- That the Good News about Jesus' sacrificial death and resurrection — the greatest display of love ever given — would be published freely to Beijingers. *"Since we are God's offspring we ought not to think that the deity is like gold or silver or stone, an image formed by the art and imagination of mortals. While God has overlooked the times of human ignorance, now he commands all people everywhere to repent, because he has fixed a day on which he will have the world judged in righteousness by a man whom he has appointed, and of this he has given assurance to all by raising him from the dead"* Acts 17:29-31 (NRSV).

• That God would be upheld as the author of salvation and the city fathers would look to Him for its plans of defense and protection. *"Instead of bronze I will bring gold, instead of iron I will bring silver; instead of wood, bronze, instead of stones, iron. I will appoint Peace as your overseer and Righteousness as your taskmaster. Violence shall no more be heard in your land, devastation or destruction within your borders; you shall call your walls Salvation and your gates Praise"* Isaiah 60:17,18 (NRSV).

• That countless songs of God's love would be sung over the city of Beijing and there would be many festivals in celebration of this. *"Sing aloud, O daughter of Zion; shout, O Israel! Rejoice and exult with all your heart, O daughter of Jerusalem! The Lord, your God, is in your midst, a warrior who gives victory; he will rejoice over you with gladness, he will renew you in His love; he will exult over you with loud singing as on a day of festival"* Zephaniah 3:14,17 (NRSV).

CHAPTER THREE

Repentance and Humility

*"If My people who are called by My name shall **humble themselves**, pray, seek, crave and require of necessity My face, and **turn from their wicked ways**, then will I hear from Heaven, forgive their sin, and heal their land"*
2 Chronicles 7:14 (AMP) (Emphasis mine).

What intimate language the Lord used to show His tenderness toward Beijing! The last prophecy of the previous meeting had used these words from scripture which originally revealed God's fathomless love for Jerusalem.

> *"O, Jerusalem, Jerusalem, murdering the prophets and stoning those who are sent to you! How often would I have gathered your children together as a mother fowl gathers her brood under her wings and you refused..."* Matthew 23:37 (AMP).

In these words we find Jerusalem a holy and deeply loved city of God, even despite its rejection of Love. Here we see a reflection of what the Father's unreserved love for other cities of the world might be like. That that love is probably different though correspondingly deep is a truth we have already seen, for it is a scriptural theme that God loves cities. In fact through Jesus' words, we see the nurturing heart of the Father waiting and desiring to draw the city to Himself. No matter how it has failed in rebellion He wants to love the city out of its hurt and pain to healing and prosperity. Just as a mother hen will give her own life for her chicks, so the Lord Jesus has offered the ultimate sacrifice for the city (its people and the land) that salvation, safety, comfort and shelter would be found under His wings.

Hearts of Love?

In the weeks that followed our repentance for the sins of our forefathers, I noticed my desire to see large numbers of Chinese become part of God's family grew much stronger. There was also an awareness that the Lord was watching all my relationships with them. The Father had shown us His incredible heart of love for the city, but what about us, His servants? Did our lifestyle match our prayer?

I began to notice little happenings and my reactions to them. There were those multitudinous passings through school gates and all the while being watched, the times I was cheated and charged a price far higher than the Chinese themselves would pay, because I was a foreigner. Sometimes it was the 'tough' attitude inside me pulsing out terse words when a taxi driver seemed to charge more than usual. At other times frustrations mounted when asking for something to be fixed that took "a month of Mondays" and then often it was not fixed at all. Of course the language barrier didn't help much, but frequently it felt like a concrete wall and there were enough of those around already! Honestly, it was hard to know where you stood with any locals! Wondering what the game was, I asked myself what was so different about living here.

It's clear now, that I didn't understand much about the Chinese way-of-doing-things nor their love of rules. You could call it culture shock, part of the adjustment process. I had spent a year in Taiwan in preparation to face cultural differences, however, it was that "on-line with God" feeling *again,* that pulled me up short. Suddenly I knew that the way I handled every one of these situations was a key issue with Him. It wasn't what happened to me but how I treated *people* that mattered to the Lord. Did I show them His unconditional love? I remembered sharing with the prayer strategy group some points from Cindy Jacobs' book *Possessing the Gates of the Enemy (*Creation House). Her teaching was an excellent reminder to me now. In our role as intercessors we had no right to any rights. No right to get angry, no right to our own time, no right to be right, no right to contend for that right.

Convicted, I sheepishly made a resolution to help the next Chinese person who asked for help. The request came from a student poor in English who wanted some private, weekly tutoring. There *was* a place in my heavy schedule! In some ways I wondered what difference helping one person would make when millions of English students needed a helping hand, (not that I had any other plans to help!) There is no doubt the tutoring did make something of a difference for *this* only child in whom family, friends and teachers had invested so much hope for their future.

In fact God's message for me at the time required that I drink my own medicine and learn to help one person at a time, that I do good and show love to individuals. Father wanted me to learn to give His love away. On the schedule for me was a crash course in forgiveness, *including* the practicum — repentance. Some of the principles I learnt are foundational to this chapter on repentance and humility.

Forgiveness

What is so important about understanding forgiveness? It may seem a compromise to avoid embarrassment or loss of face, as the Chinese say. It's quite the opposite! I learned that forgiveness is not agreeing with the wrong done, not condoning it, nor becoming a doormat but rather releasing the other party and what they have done, to God. It's safe to let go and set people free to the Father — He really understands, loves with integrity and judges without bias. Judging is His job not ours.

Judgments

A big component of living out forgiveness is learning not to judge other people by our own standards. We tend to judge by what we see, by external human standards. Isn't it easy to set ourselves up as a measuring stick that others must reach? We can think everyone else is wrong and we are right! Jesus said that He didn't judge (or condemn or sentence) anyone (John 8:15). When we do this we are trying to be higher than Jesus, the just Judge. We effectively put ourselves higher than the law. In reality, judging, sentencing and condeming people only puts us "under" the law and subject to greater judgments. (We also come "under" the people we have spoken out about.) It's very hard to forgive when we are holding to judgments of others.

The Law

Understanding that the same law established to bring blessings could also bring cursing to my life settled the issue for me! It is the law that acts as schoolmaster to bring us to Christ. Yes, if we walk in the principles of the law of God there will be abundant blessings. Yet if we break the laws of the universe, the same laws can release cursing (Deuteronomy 28:1-2,15). By sinning we effectively come "under" the law. What does that mean? Let me explain by a comparison.

The devil traffics in law — he is always accusatory, always negative, always condemning. God, however, traffics in grace. He is always positive, always comforts, encourages and loves us. When we love our enemies and are kind and forgiving towards them (as God is) we walk in grace, above the law. Conversely, to walk under the law is to be subject to the law, or the presence of accusation, condemnation, fault finding, the demanding of rights and negativity in our lives. This is entry to the legal court system of the devil. Do I need to say it is the way down? God loves us so much that He doesn't demand anything. Even concerning *this walk* He gives us a choice! The truth to grasp is that *we are the ones who set blessings or curses into motion.*

Forgiveness starts the healing of our own hurt, and is proportionately more essential for us than other parties involved. The reason is that when forgiveness from our hearts is a choice true love begins, as does the road to freedom and destiny. This old saying puts it so well: "Forgiveness is to set a prisoner free and find the prisoner was you!" On the other hand forgiveness towards the other party releases the Holy Spirit and God's angels to work in the other's life. It's saying, *"I let that person go without judging — He's yours Lord. Thank you for what You're doing in that life. I'm now asking you, O God, to forgive that person."* The outworking of forgiveness includes praying the Father's blessing on others despite their critical words, rejection or hurtful ways. Let me illustrate with a story.

Some time ago I was asked to work closely with other colleagues on a concert production. In previous productions I had found it difficult to work with Chinese, even in simple procedures. Instructions were interpreted differently and completed at changed deadlines but there was not much communication with me. Having begun to use the principles as dialogued above, I felt hopeful about the results this time. Now, I had been given authority to get the needed support from whomever it was necessary. Everything seemed to work well until I met Victoria. She had other ideas which would have been fine, but as director, I felt this would not produce the best performance. Every time she disagreed I said I would think about her ideas and let her know the next day. At home I prayed for her, forgave her and asked blessing for her in every area of her life. Then I remembered that others had suffered offence through my own inflexibility and so began repentance for my own sin and judgments on others. I continued to ask blessing for her. This continued for several days but we weren't in agreement about the way ahead until I asked another colleague whose opinion I trusted, what I should do. At this point I was willing to use Victoria's ideas, but my trusted colleague suggested making my own decision and sticking with it. Before going back to Victoria I prayed once again, forgiving and asking for the Father's richest blessing on her. That day when I presented my decision, she finally agreed. What happened? In fact Victoria followed my instructions. The result was that her part of the concert was rated the best and *she* was appraised as such, also.

That was when I realised that what Victoria really wanted all along was to get the best results, to be considered and made to feel important. Perhaps this "love" had never been given her sufficiently at other times in her life, hence the passion to have her way. Father had not only answered my prayer for her, but had changed my heart, forgiven and caused me to remain in grace. When I heard Victoria's news I felt my spirit was so free it could fly!!

Grace

A lifestyle of blessing and offering mercy to others keeps us in grace. We earlier talked about forgiveness as meaning to let go. Particularly when offences come forgiveness provides an escape from the power of the offence to take us down to the negative court system of judgment. Jesus said some straight-up stuff about loving those who give us a hard time (Luke 6:35,36). I must admit it's not easy to give someone another coat when they lost the last one. Neither is it easy in a busy schedule to give time to people who seem to waste it. Now I understand that Jesus' admonitions were to help us reap His blessings in even the most unlikely circumstances. We have to keep on blessing others in the hard times.

Responses of forgiveness and blessing towards others will allow us to harvest mercy when it's needed, but responses of negativity will incur a reaping of the hard times we have given others. There is no law against laughter, nor giving away love, acts of kindness, forgiveness and mercy nor even explaining the truth (with compassion), also an expression of real love. Living in grace is a place above the law where no enemy can get us! As James 2:13 says, mercy triumphs over judgment.

Speaking honestly, these deeper principles about forgiveness, judgment, law and grace are things about which I have gained a fuller perspective since the strategy in 1994.[2] Having realised my shortcomings, I felt for a while that I had let the Lord down somehow, for I had not been as pure in heart as He would have wanted. How grateful I am that the Lord's ways are higher than ours. As I now know, every prayer of forgiveness for another (even *that* they don't forgive or are unable to acknowledge faults) does spiritual warfare. Forgiveness is interceding on another's behalf. Eventually I could see that this work of the Holy Spirit had been effective in others and me, for *as much as I had forgiven in prayer, my life had been and was being changed, too.*

---

[2] Teaching from the following ministries are recommended in this regard. John and Paula Sandford, *Renewal of the Mind* (Victory House Publishers, Tulsa Oklahoma, 1991,) also *Transformation of the Inner Man* (Victory House Publishers,Tulsa Oklahoma, 1982) and their leadership seminars and other books; John and Carol Arnott *The Importance of Forgiveness* (Soverign World, 1997); Jack Frost, Audio Tapes especially the series "*You were Created for Love*" (Shiloh Place Ministries, P.O. BOX 5, SC 29528, USA).

Through repentance and humility the work of the Holy Spirit is double-edged, strikingly productive in both parties. On the one hand, as we (His body) repent for our sin, forgive others and stay in grace *we are healed.* Prayers of forgiveness, love and blessing towards others (even unbelievers) *open wider their heart's door* for Heaven's intervention. All of it happens though we are still in process as individuals. What wonderful weapons God has given us in repentance and forgiveness!

Counting Blessings

As foreigners for Christ in China (and anywhere) we are always closely observed and our personal reactions are monitored. Much good has been done in China. In chapter 2 we saw the origins of some issues which still affect China today. It would appear that the historical precedent of conflict has tended to make forming judgments easy. This is just the ploy our enemy can use if we fall into that way of thinking! Grace, on the other hand, has taught me to count my blessings and so see the beautiful qualities of the Chinese people.

Others who have noticed include one photographer. Heida Morrison authored a book about Old Beijingers in the first quarter of the twentieth century detailing the cheerful and uncomplaining attitude of a people suffering greatly[3]. Adding to her list of qualities, I would include resilience and dogged persistence in the midst of trouble. Many Chinese are extremely loyal and try to be kind. Beijingers also are quick to speak in their welcoming, hospitable attitude towards visitors. In many cases they go out of their way to emphasize this point.

In my opinion, one of the greatest honors you could ever receive in Beijing is to be called a "lao Beijingren", or an "Old Beijinger". I've tried to think about what it really means since there is no way

---

[3] Hedda Morrison *A Photographer in Old Beijing* (New York USA, Oxford University Press 1985, 1993) p.7

this title could be really true for any foreigner. It's impossible to get a visa to last twenty to thirty years, for one thing. It can never mean that you speak Chinese like the natives do! (There is no way you will unless you were brought up speaking Chinese!) Neither can it mean that you've identified yourself fully in cultural aspects, as you could never completely lose your own cultural identity. Rather, receiving such a term is a recognition of your efforts towards these goals. It's a compliment, a statement of acceptance, and let me say, it works! To me, receiving such a "title" is no small privilege.

Some days I have been very grateful for their sensitivity. For example, a Chinese doctor is extremely gentle and medical check-ups are a breeze — so much so that even injections don't hurt! People with great depth of character are among some of my best friends. Their stories of bravery astound me. When their full life histories are told, I usually conclude my own sufferings to be nothing at all.

Some issues inevitably come up in everyday life. Let me cite an example.

Yesterday I was carrying a light metal bookcase home. The salesman had kindly offered to assemble the kit for me in the shop and here I was almost home. Inside the large gate of the compound, a lady dismounted from her bike, intimated that she was going my way and invited me to put the bookcase on her bike carrier. Gladly accepting the offer, I did as she suggested. I learnt of her proposed trip overseas next year and her expressed concern about receiving help when in the strange new country. She said that we all need to help each other in this world. In her last sentence the lady made an interesting comment. The Chinese don't often help us [the foreigners] because they think we have a motive. Of course I assured her that this wasn't the case, yet hoped like anything she would have plenty of "good care" experiences from other foreigners she meets.

I felt so blessed to have received this act of kindness and trust though it included defense! As someone else once told me, the old fear that the white man has come to China to "hunt and get his prey" still lurks near the surface. Keeping an open mind, blessing and showing love (the best that I can) to each person I meet is the least I can do. Things misunderstood at the time often become clear later. *We each have to make the choice to bless,* (far beyond it seems reasonable) for we must pray that this cycle of pain and associated misunderstandings will be entirely broken.

Stories of encounter with others may seem trivial but they represent important issues. There are two sides to every relationship and often incorrect ways of relating on both sides of cross-cultural encounters. Many foreigners say they learn a lot of patience in Beijing. (Indeed, prayer is the only way forward!) Can you see the need though, to deal with pride and arrogance in order to become real servants in the Spirit of Christ's love? While we all need to make decisions, a tendency to pass judgment on others — without letting go, or manifesting forgiveness — could be something to submit to the Lord.

The challenges of living in China have been like God's sandpaper to expose the bad fruit — the result of bad seed I once sowed in my life. We will talk about the law of sowing and reaping in another chapter but just now I'll say that in dealing with my own life's issues, I discovered the same keys were effective in reaping peace in cross-cultural conflict. Somewhere along the way I learned the importance of repentance and forgiveness as a lifestyle and as a means of dealing with destructive patterns in the Chinese environment.

Looking back now, it was when willing to repent *corporately* with others for the heaped up sins of my forefathers towards China, that a process of healing began in my own life. (And following our corporate repentance we were released to do identificational repentance for the Chinese.) It's certainly true that I have done more repenting in China than in my whole life previously! In fact, the

Spirit of God has brought more revelations about repentance to the church since the early 1990's. Now it is common to hear about repentance being yielded between corporate groups, cities and nations as well as individuals and families.

Repentance

Repentance (a change of mind and heart, with a hatred of past sin echoed in a change of behaviour), is the real condition that means God *will* answer our prayers for healing of the nations. The verse quoted at the beginning of the chapter is a crucial mooring for us in the sea of repentance and prayer. Let's look at that again:

> *"If My people who are called by My name shall* ***humble themselves,*** *pray, seek, crave and require of necessity My face, and* ***turn from their wicked ways****, then will I hear from Heaven, forgive their sin, and heal their land"* (2 Chronicles 7:14, AMP) (Emphasis added).

So much is contained in this verse that we will return to study it. Primarily though, God is addressing our need to repent during our prayer for the healing of nations. Individually we must *turn away* from our sin for then God will answer our prayers. (We must personally be anchored in truth when the storms arise, as they will.) This promise is stated in the plural. I believe it is individually *and corporately* that we must take time to repent and pray for the healing of nations.

Individual Repentance

Firstly, our individual lifestyle is vital. To serve rather than control, to forgive rather than accuse, to praise rather than find fault, to smile rather than frown, to find out the truth rather than believe a lie (even if it's commonly believed), to offer mercy rather than judgment, in all these we are choosing to turn from our wicked ways. Jesus compared good deeds and moral excellence [lifestyle] to a lighthouse that shines out into the dark. Such light cannot be quenched. This landmark of lifestyle that honors God and brings His praise wherever we go can be a powerful arsenal of spiritual warfare.

Secondly, we need to pray together — corporately — for the city in which we live, seeking its prosperity and identifying with its sins in repentance.

Corporate Repentance — Prayers for Groups

My thoughts of how to pray for Beijing were guided by biblical prayers of Moses, Stephen and Daniel. They all asked for the Lord's remittance of sins committed by *groups* and in the process *identified themselves* with the people they represented. Nowdays leaders of intercession call this identificational repentance.

Moses didn't waste words when he asked the Lord to forgive the Israelites (Ex 32:11,30-32); he said he wanted his name out of heaven's archives if God didn't forgive them! Moses even put his relationship with God on the line! What an example of determined identification!

Stephen pleaded forgiveness for those who stoned him (Acts 7:60)! His prayer would seem to have borne fruit in the life of one of those within earshot. Saul of Tarsus who originally approved the stoning later had an encounter with the Lord Jesus Christ and became Paul the apostle.

Daniel was an upright and devout man who didn't personally contribute to the nation's original sins, yet he identified with the outworking of its judgment which directly affected his future — or lack of it! As well, he was linked with national sins of the past through his nationality. He repented and entreated forgiveness for Israel's sins using plural nouns such as "we" and "us". He also asked for mercy to avert the devastation of Jerusalem as had been prophesied. He assumed his responsibility seriously and was very specific in *what* he repented for (See Daniel 9:11,13,14).

The way that Jesus prayed in gentleness for the city of Jerusalem is awesome, but it developed through time spent in prayer. He had trudged over many parts of the capital and knew the issues people faced intricately enough to give provocative and authoritative challenges about many of life's issues. He loved the city, cradling and carrying it close to his heart. In all these ways He became intimately identified with it — a huge act of humility. It was along this path of identification that led Jesus to Jerusalem and the cross. It was there that He spoke to His Father and said:

> *"Father forgive them, for they know not what they do"* (Luke 23:34, AMP).

I take this petition to mean He was asking the Father that *their* part in the decision and perpetration of His crucifixion — the murder of an innocent man — would not be held against them. Jesus initiated forgiveness toward the city authorities — the *group* of people who had committed sins against Him individually and corporately — while He was still suffering. The cross is our ultimate model of God's identification with humanity. The cross calls us to walk across dividing lines of culture, race and people groups with humility and prayer.

"If", We Repent

Our willingness to follow the example of Jesus, the Head, and join others in His body who will stand in the gap in repentance for cities and nations is a personal choice. It appears that it *is* a specific call, as some in Christ's body do not hear the invitation of 2 Chronicles 7:14. As Daniel received a revelation from scripture (in Daniel 9), of how intrinsic his repentance was to the nation's future and his own life, he was empowered to identify specifically in repentance. It was following his fasting and repentance prayers for the nation that an angel sent from Heaven told Daniel of breakthrough and things to come. The call to prayer for nations is to those God specifically assigns this task and they will know who they are. We must get our instructions directly from God for our lives.

In identificational repentance we are interceding for those who cannot acknowledge their sin or even respond to forgiveness. Even as Jesus prayed in Luke 23:34, we are asking God to remit the sins of those persons who are disreputable and unworthy. Jesus forgave the repentant criminal who was crucified alongside him. His forgiveness of this man who had sinned while he was without Christ calls us to intercede in like manner for others. After He rose from the dead and appeared to His disciples for the first time as they were gathered together, Jesus had three things to say. He firstly greeted them with peace and prayed for them to receive the Holy Spirit, and then He said:

> *"..if you forgive the sins of any one they are forgiven; if you retain the sins of any one, they are retained"* (John 20:23, AMP).

This was such an important key for them that Jesus talked about it on this first reunion with them! Do we grasp, I wonder, the responsibility invested in and expected of us in this verse? It's a sobering thought that our remittance of the sins of others (or lack of remittance) can greatly bless or greatly hinder.

Someone once asked me about the people who go on doing evil in the city even after intercessors have repented and pleaded with God on their behalf. Identificational repentance is a first step that only God's people — not politicians, not social reformers, nor counselors — can do for others who don't know Him. The job of intercession for cities, nations and people groups is not demanding things of God, but rather our answer to His call for humility and repentance (2 Chronicles 7:14). I also believe that individuals must sooner or later confess their own sins. Firstly however they must hear the Good News personally, though stories of supernatural encounters resulting in conversions to Christ are occuring around the world. If we answer the call to intercession, identifying with peoples, cities and nations in repentance, God will hear and heal according to the promise of His Word. We must not give up, but rather worship Him as Lord!

Our Identification Process

In the process of our prayer and research we began to *get to know* the people and their capital, so understanding more of their struggles, burdens and mindsets than before. Nobody knows the suffering of another until he's lived in their shoes. Though we could never deny our own identity, living in the city and *having a reason to observe it*, gave us a front-row look at what life is really like for them. That was extremely important, especially because of our cross-cultural vista. We began to see parts of the city we never knew existed before, and learn about its history. I believe this *getting acquainted* identification process was part of the call to prayer for the city, and a part of seeing the real issues faced by the local people. Meaningful repentance could come no other way.

For those of us in the prayer teams committed to research, the identification process involved a lot of foot-work; trailing unknown city streets, finding dusty places of antiquity and asking many questions. All credit be given, too, to those researchers who worked with tight timetables! Surprised by how much they committed themselves to, they told about the real grace they were given to accomplish all the work, service and other commitments of life. Each person helped to reach the intermediary goals of research that finally helped us piece together the big picture. The willingness of the team indicated the sense of privilege many felt to do God's bidding — to help love a city to healing through prayer.

Identificational Repentance

It means "walking in their shoes" until we can specifically identify corporate sins, asking the Lord to forgive, and praying for the cleansing power of His blood. Could we truly repent for the sins of the people? What if it included repenting for sins of bloodshed? (The shedding of innocent blood pollutes the land and brings a curse on the land and its people [2 Chronicles 7:13,14; Deuteronomy 21]. These sins come up before God as a stench in His nostrils, though He doesn't want any to perish. Nevertheless, He is dependent on His people answering His call to bridge the gap between the corporate historical sins and His pending judgment for those sins — in repentance [Isaiah 59:1-16]).

Some Repentance for the sins of the Capital

At this time the Lord drew my attention to six main ways the shedding of blood had taken place. These were doorways which had brought much wounding to the people and the land. Our intecessory group meeting was held the weekend before the fifth anniversary of the June 4, 1989 incident in Tiananmen Square. This meeting (the fifth in the project), was not specifically arranged to coincide with this date, it just happened that way.

Our team meeting commenced with loud praise and worship. This phase culminated in a remarkable hush; quite an indication of the Lord's presence. Finding myself restrained as though set in concrete, I understood that the Lord was setting the tone for this meeting. We waited for some time before I asked another leader whether they felt it was OK to go on. It seemed God was getting our attention, powerfully presiding over this meeting. It wasn't hard to tell He was very interested. After a while we gradually went on.

In the preparation for the time of repentance, the team pray-ers were instructed to find one of the six topics they felt especially drawn to. Six groups formed and began to review the issues at hand. I have listed the things we repented of that day in obedience to the Lord.

Topic #1 — Bloodshed in Tiananmen Square, June 4, 1989 We asked God's forgiveness for the large numbers of people who were killed, and entered into repentance for death on both sides of the conflict. (To read what others have documented about specific worldviews held at the time see the reference below[3].)

Topic #2 — Bloodshed during the Cultural Revolution, 1966 to 1976 We especially repented for the tremendous loss of life. As the nation's capital, Beijing was the birthplace of the Revolution and the huge cost to the people began with what was termed a "battle".[4] Again, we were led to repent for both "sides" of the populace. As well, we repented (and including the June 4 "days"), for choices made to deny facts and therefore grief, the process of coming to terms with great losses to the collective identity of the city, nation, groups and families.

Topic #3 — Suicide — Our repentance included this area which has been a common way of dealing with difficult situations over centuries. I list the historical facts below, to help

---

[3] Harrison E. Salisbury, *The New Emperors* (Hammersmith, London, HarperCollins Publishers) p. 38

[4] Ibid., p. 121

others in prayer.[5]

Topic #4 — Abortion — Our repentance for the killing of the unborn *in utero* was not a new concept. Though statistically difficult to prove, that it does occur on a massive scale has been documented by many.[6]

Topic #5 — Infanticide and Selling Children as Slaves This time our repentance was for babies, unwanted toddlers and young children who were killed at birth or sold to whomever would pay. Conditions in the orphanages (which have received some overseas aid) are greatly improved today and are now better than before the Cultural Revolution. The traditional preference for a boy rather than a girl is still noticeable, thus the need for our repentance and prayer.[7]

Topic #6 — Human Sacrifice — Repentance specifically included countless struggles in the Forbidden City which had brought bloodshed. Other documented accounts that occurred before the twentieth century, are listed below.[8]

5* During Mongolian rule, people chose to commit suicide rather than face life under foreign rule. The story is told of a Song General who was captured by the Mongolians and offered freedom in exchange for his loyal service as a high official. The general replied that he would rather be put to death than to serve any other than the Song Dynasty. His wish was granted. Madge Huntington, *A Traveller's Guide to Chinese History* (New York, USA, Henry Holt & Company 1987) pp 93,97

*Many suicides occurred within the walls of the Forbidden City. During the Qing Dynasty alone (1644-1912), the throne received news of two thousand cases of suicide among bondservants of families of noblemen, bureaucrats and landlords every year. The reasons given were lack of proper education and material comforts, physical torment accentuated by cold and hunger. It was stated *then* that this had become an inevitable trend. Er Si, Shang Hongkui and Others, Trans., by Zhao Shuhan *Inside Stories of the Forbidden City* (Beijing, China, New World Press, 1986) p. 64

*Under feudalism it was the right of the landlord to kill any servant he felt was not useful. Servants would rather commit suicide than be killed by the landlord. This way of handling the problem could often be seen as an extension of a cultural practice of displaying hatred towards a person through suicide or a threat of suicide. Lucian W. Pye *China, An Introduction* (Boston, Toronto, Little Brown and Company) p. 206 Also documented by Nathan Leites in *On Violence in China* (D-20517-PR (Santa Monica, Calif: Rand, July 15, 1970)

*During the Cultural Revolution there were places such as lakes and stretches of railway lines which became known as suicide spots.

*When the Japanese were defeated on Chinese soil, many of them committed suicide

This was a powerful time of repentance for the sins of the city and nation. We asked God's forgiveness for the sins of the "victims" and the "perpetrators" of the sins. It turned out to be something one couldn't do lightly. In repentance we became aware of our partial attitudes. Though not agreeing with the wrong done it was another thing to forgive the instigators of wrong and suffering. Could we truly forgive? Really identifying now, there was nothing we could do but plead God's mercy for all of us! We pleaded for yokes to be broken and captives to go free. As small group prayer culminated one person from each of the six groups was invited to pray in repentance, asking God's forgiveness. When the prayers ended, the room grew very still and for the second time that day God's presence fell *heavily*. It was so strong that again, we were constrained as though held in check, to be still and wait on the Lord.

As we sat, the Lord gave me a picture of a huge man with his chest bared. The focal point of this picture was a colossal wound directly over his heart. In fact the skin was peeled back, the arter-

---

rather than surrender.

6 *Family News from Dr James Dobson* (CO, USA, Focus on the Family, Issue No. 9, 1997) p.2 Patrick J. StG Johnstone, *Operation World* (Zondervan Publishing House, Grand Rapids, Michigan) p. 165

7 *Family News from Dr James Dobson* (CO., USA, Focus on the Family, Issue NO. 9, 1997) p.2

8 *During the writing of the book, I felt there was something important we had missed in our repentance under this topic. I asked the Lord to help me get it right. Within two weeks, I was told of a new book just published in English. Though amazed at the timing of the publication, this timing emphasized the importance of specific repentance in the Lord's eyes. In obedience to Him I did repent for the sins of bloodshed as detailed in this story. The story told of 12 palace maids and their unsuccessful attempt to assassinate the Emperor Jiajing (1522-1566). The maids were seriously threatened due to the Emperor's obsession with making immortality pills with parts of their bodies. Despite the attack on his life, the Emperor continued to take longevity pills and twice during his reign ordered the selection of increasingly younger girls from Beijing and elsewhere. A total of 460 girls between eight and fourteen were drafted. Er Si,Shang Hongkui and Others, Trans. by Zhao Shuhan, *Inside Stories of the Forbidden city* (Beijing, China, New World Press, 1986) pp.29-33 This book is not intended to be a comprehensive list of historical bloodshed in the city!

*There is reliable record that human sacrifice occurred at two of the altars in Beijing. Robert Storey, *Beijing City Guide* (Hong Kong, Lonely Planet Publications, 1966) p. 162

ies of his heart were visible and there was blood everywhere. I could hear his heart beating but there seemed to be something wrong; it was an irregular heartbeat. This man was fighting for his life. Almost as soon as the vision came to an end, the understanding was given to me. The man was an embodiment of China and its wounded heart was Beijing. The whole nation was in a precarious situation because of its heart condition.

As I stood and shared the vision, we prayed together for the breaking of the curse over the land. We asked in Jesus' name that every demonic principality that had come through these doorways would be dispossessed and gone from the land and its people. We asked for a cleansing of the blood of Jesus, specifically requesting that the doors would remain closed to these powers should they try to return. The timing of this prayer in relation to the next weekend, the anniversary of June 4, 1989 now seemed so significant.

June 4, 1994 did pass without incident, as far as we could tell. In fact if you asked what happened as a result of our prayer (and the prayers of others in ensuing years) I could only say that I'll have to wait until we see re-play videos in Heaven to find out what further bloodshed and judgment of God was averted as a result. I do know that God presenced Himself powerfully and walked with us through the repentance. That reality is enough for me!

There are two important reasons the Lord has had for the publication of this chapter. Firstly, bloodshed has occured all over China and not just in Beijing. It is a reminder of the pressing responsibility we have to repent and to pray for cleansing. Secondly, a clear understanding of how, why and when the sin occurred is essential, for specific identification. God's people must graple with reality, release emotions and express grief, for then repentance will be real. Issues will be resolved. God *will* cleanse and heal our lands. He awaits our prayer.

While you ponder the contents of this chapter and perhaps begin prayers of repentance for your country, be encouraged to know the blessing of cleansing. As we repent for our people and our land, asking for the blood of Jesus to cleanse, we also receive purification from sins' defilement in the burden-bearing process.

PRAYER POINTS

• That Beijing would become a city where upright standards are championed, where (as Ted Haggard says), "it's hard to go to hell from." *"Go through, go through the gates, prepare the way for the people; build up, build up the highway, clear it of stones, lift up an ensign over the peoples"* (Isaiah 62:10, NRSV). *"Is not this the fast that I choose: to loose the bonds of injustice, to undo the thongs of the yoke, to let the oppressed go free, and to break every yoke"* (Isaiah 58:6, NRSV)?

• That many Chinese intercessors, watchmen and leaders will receive deliverance and healing and this will become like a river sweeping over the land. *"Do not remember against us the iniquities of our ancestors: let your compassion come speedily to meet us, for we are brought very low. Help us, O God of our salvation, for the glory of your name; deliver us, and forgive our sins, for your name's sake ...."* (Psalm 79:8-10, NRSV).

• That many more anointed servants of God will bring healing to the Chinese until Beijing is a place where Isaiah 61:1-4 is a reality for millions of people. *"The Spirit of the Lord has anointed me; he has sent me to bring good news to the oppressed, to bind up the brokenhearted, to proclaim liberty to the captives, and release to the prisoners; to proclaim the year of the Lord's favour, and the day of vengeance of our God; to comfort all who mourn; to provide for those who mourn in Zion — to give them a garland instead of ashes, the oil of gladness instead of mourning, the mantle of praise instead of a faint spirit. They will be called oaks of righteousness, the planting of the Lord, to display your glory. They shall build up the ancient ruins, they shall raise up the former devastations; they shall repair the ruined cities, the devastations of many generations"* (NRSV).

CHAPTER FOUR

Pulling Down the High Places

'That night the Lord said to him, "Take your father's bull, the second bull seven years old, and ***pull down*** *the altar of Baal that your father has, and* ***cut down*** *the Asherah that is beside it; And* ***build an altar to the Lord your God*** *on top of this stronghold, with stones laid in proper order; then take the second bull, and offer a burnt sacrifice with the wood of the Asherah which you shall cut down"* (Judges 6:25-26, AMP), [Emphasis added].

Now, at the end of the fifth group meeting on Sunday May 29, we had two weeks to go before our 'Gideon's Day'. As early as the beginning of April, the Lord had signaled me back to Gideon and his orders to pull down the altar of Baal. I received similar instructions about Beijing. (The visits to the altars began in April but were spread out to May 29. In this chapter the altar-visits follow each other in unbroken sequence, but please see the time line [Appendix E] for their chronological order with other events.)

A conversation fragment remembered from Taiwan days got my attention. "Beijing has seven altars." How often had the resonating signals in my brain archives gone off before something *clicked* into place? I couldn't recall exactly but the Holy Spirit was connecting things together. He showed me that this aspect of Gideon's story was helpful in seeing more of the spiritual "big picture" for Beijing. Actually, I woudn't have believed the report about these altars in such modern times if I hadn't happened to find one of them by chance on my first visit to Beijing in 1991. Then, I didn't see the public signs informing visitors what it was, but I can still remember how the Holy Spirit whispered to me — "This is an altar." He had a good reason for alerting my attention, of that I was sure. This was the Altar of Land and Grain, which consisted of a raised platform with a small pyramid-shaped obelisk in the middle with five colors of sand representating five varieties of grain. I stayed long enough to read the description of what it was, and walking out of the park I found a sign saying "To Altar". It confirmed what I had already heard from the Holy Spirit. We would pray twice over this altar in obedience to the Lord, but more about that later. Now in April 1994 God was asking us to "do a Gideon" on the altars. What did He mean?

Gideon's Altar-razing Night

The order to pull down the high place came before Gideon went to battle for his city and nation. First of all *he* had to move into a right place with God. He had to cleanse his own turf and make sure there was nothing out there in the field that could come between him and God. Gideon obliterated the image and altar on his father's land, closing the open door to the demon power in his life and unbarring the doorway to God's power. (He burned a sacrifice on a fresh altar in the same spot to dedicate this place to God). Then he could defeat the enemy.

This was not a new truth for me. In the tropical islands of the Pacific where my parents worked when I was a child the local people had strange worship festivals. Our family would usually read

Bible stories together before going to sleep. On those festival nights, against the backdrop of weird sounds going on well into the night, we continued our practice. My deep questions about the local people were answered as we read the stories. It must have been the Holy Spirit that taught me God didn't like His people having idols around in their homes or cities because even as a child I could remember many examples of the Israelites' defeat. The lessons were reinforced through my environment. Since those years the Lord has underlined the importance of giving first place to Him, even by what possessions we have at home (Leviticus 26:1, Deuteronomy 7:25,26, 1 Chronicles 14:12). Lifestyle, a form of worship, must acknowledge Him *as* the Lord of Lords or there is no power over the enemy.

Personal Application

This is why I knew when God told us to pull down the high places as part of the prayer strategy there was a personal application as there had been for Gideon. We had a time of searching through our possessions (books, jewelry, paintings, clothing, cultural artifacts, carvings, toys and gifts) to get rid of things not honoring to the Lord. We asked questions such as, "What articles are in this home that don't honor You Lord?", "Which ones violate our respect for You as Lord of Lords?", "Are there evil spirits that other occupants have welcomed that You want to leave?" With the process begun, the Holy Spirit led us on in His time.

City/Nation-Wide Application

Gideon's obedience was strategic in God's eyes. It seems the altar and image had been erected on Gideon's father's land in co-operation with the city leaders. In fact the Almighty's directives to Gideon to destroy the altar and pole are amplified as this 'Baal' would have been hailed "lord of the city"[1]. It is a title implying territorial tenure.

Where once there had been a league transacted between city leaders and a demonic entity, Gideon's altar-razing and altar-building ceremonies reclaimed the site for God. There were ramifications for personal and city-wide victory, too (Judges 6:27,28).

Transactions made at altars are different from covenants made between people, in that they are between people and their so-called "gods". Such making of leagues, transactions and covenants invoked a curse on the people, firstly, when demonic powers behind the idols are given free reign and secondly, when leagues were broken. No wonder the townsmen in Gideon's day were worried!

The High Places

The Holy Spirit's leading to pray over the high places in Beijing was as strategic for us as Gideon's instructions were for him. A high place is a geographical site set apart for worship of gods where the shedding of innocent human or animal blood has occurred. So doing, people covenant with demon powers to become empowered by them, knowingly or unknowingly inviting a greater darkness to their lives and to the city. The Lord cares! He wanted to bring remittance of these sins, at least if His instructions to us to go to these places were anything to go by. His directions became quite significant when we learned that many state ceremonies over the centuries had been held at each of the altar sites. The book, *In Search of Old Peking,* confirmed that these rituals were deemed necessary for the continuance of the four seasons, planting and harvest cycles and the smooth running of the nation.

Of course we could not remove the altars like Gideon did but we could repent for the shedding of innocent blood, ask the Lord's forgiveness for the sins of idolatry, then pray for cleansing of the

---

[1] The original meaning of 'the Baal' was not the 'lord of the worshipper' but a possessor of a territory or district and the local Baalim were identified by adding the name of a particular place. See William Robertson Smith, *The Religion of the Semites: The Fundamental Institutions* (New York Schocken, 1972) pp 92, 94-96.

land to break curses from the people. We also believed for promises the Lord would give us for each site.

Scheduling a visit to each of the altar sites was key but our timetables were already overflowing. Yet, in obedience to the Lord to pull down the high places before our 'Gideon Day' these visits *had* to be completed before June 12. It was quite a feat to find friends able to accompany me on these visits to the altars. I'll recount the first two altar-visits and then the fourth altar site in detail, where there was an unexpected breakthrough.

First Altar-visit

Mary and I had taken two weeks to research, pray and ask questions in the preparation for this trip on Saturday, April 16.

Altar of Heaven At least historically, this altar was considered most significant throughout China. Built in 1420, for centuries the temple enclosure was open one day a year and access to this altar was given only to the emperor and his entourage. The stated purpose of the sacrifice he performed yearly was to ensure the continuation of nature's cycles, and was made to one the Chinese called literally, sky or heaven. It has been loosely translated to mean "father".[2] The emperor always performed this sacrifice and because of its great importance he would stay up all night in preparation for the dawn ceremony.

---

2 This being in the heavens is in modern times attributed with power over movement of yin and yang, or dualism. Here again, good and evil are equal and opposite forces, unrelated to the Christian belief where God is a loving Father who triumphed over evil and death in the person of His son, Jesus Christ. Authors of *The Mystery Confucious Couldn't Solve* propose that the first rulers of China understood religious principles which had been handed down by word of mouth since creation. By Confucius' day in 500 BC, 1700 years had passed since the first Chinese rulers and over the long passage of time a true knowledge of the Garden of Eden Border Sacrifice, part of the worship of Shang Ti, (God), had already been lost. The true meaning of the origins of the Border Sacrifice, a ceremony adhered to in the Chinese altar sacrifices, had been mislaid. Ethel R. Nelson/Richard E. Broadberry, *The Mystery Confucious Couldn't Solve* (Condordia Publishing House, St Louis, MO 1994) p. 96 It is not hard to see how a national custom without the truthful instruction of the Bible survived only as a mysterious ritual, and in time led back to occultic pathways. Our Holy Spirit led preparational intercession for the altar-visit did reflect this.

Abraham and Sarah drove Mary and me to the well-known altar positioned southern-most among the buildings of the Temple of Heaven enclosure. Sarah prayed for us in the car. We were thankful for that, as our arrival that morning found crowds of people taking photos and shooting video cameras on the top level of the three-tiered altar. Everyone seemed bent on accomplishing one feat — to stand on the round slab of marble in the centre of the altar's topmost terrace. We prayed to be able to stand on that spot (probably where animals were sacrificed) and suddenly the round slab of stone emptied entirely! We three jumped on it immediately and began to pray simultaneously, all of us making the best use of this brief but precious time. I can't remember everything I prayed but at least part of my prayer was to ask God to forgive sin and break the hold of demonic power invoked during blood sacrifices of yesteryear. The audience stood around for that brief minute dumbstruck, as if mute! It was comforting to know that though hearing our words, this Asian group would not comprehend.

As we stepped away the previous heaviness and confusion in the vicinity had indeed broken. The three of us praying all at once was a form of unity and agreement — now the job was done. I remember this verse as God's promise and sealing of the breakthrough.

> *"And though one might prevail against another, two will withstand one. A threefold cord is not quickly broken"* (Ecclesiastes 4:12, NRSV).

Second Altar-visit

As we prepared in prayer to go to the Altar of the Sun, Rebecca and I sat around a table in the open air. That Sunday May 15, we had just finished lunch together and I had felt so sick I could hardly eat. Rebecca's prayer helped a little but then the heaviness returned. We concluded it could be an intercessory burden. We decided to pray and repent for the sins previously committed at this altar. Although there was no written evidence, it seemed the Holy Spirit was saying there had been child sacrifice at this altar. At the very start of our prayer a spirit of repentance fell on us; weeping, we asked forgiveness for the abandonment of unwanted babies, abortion and the one-child policy. We asked God's forgiveness for the low value placed on human life and children destroyed as a result, for all such societal attitudes towards children. The burden then lifted and we made our way to the Altar of the Sun, a central point in the largest diplomatic quarter of the city.

Altar of the Sun Built in 1530, this was first called "Altar of the Rising Sun" probably related to its eastern location in the city. There was also a sign at one point in history which read "Portal to sun-spirit worship." This altar is square with a set of stairs at each of the four cardinal points and surrounded with a round red-tiled wall, the color red being symbolic of the sun. The emperor performed sacrifices only on alternate years, and appointed court officials obliged in other years for the ceremony which took place two hours before dawn.

Rebecca and I arrived in the altar enclosure to find there wasn't a soul in sight. Using oil as a symbol of the Holy Spirit's ministry, we boldly anointed the four corners of the altar. In prayer we applied the blood of Jesus over this land to cleanse away curses and asked the Lord that this large enclosure would one day become the venue of an open air crusade where the gospel would be preached. Our prayer was so straightforward and I felt a thousand times better than just after lunch. Now I had faith to believe our prayer assignment at this altar was done.

Spring Rain Two days later, on Tuesday morning, we woke with great surprise to the sound of falling rain. It was the subject of excited chatter everywhere, as I remember. The Chinese have a saying which goes *"Spring rain is as precious as oil."* The lack of spring rain as a climatic pattern is obviously old enough to have become proverbial. However we felt that the spring rain could be a sign of healing of the land following our identificational repentance and prayer at the altar. The margin of my New Revised Standard Bible says of Malachi 4:2 that the sun of righteousness refers to Jesus, the light of the world, the light of the glory of God. Remember that the first name given to this place was "Altar to the Rising Sun"? Could it be that as we repented and invited the work of the Holy Spirit, it was accepted as worship to Jesus, the Sun of Righteousness? This verse is a promise of healing, for the Hebrew word for "wings" means "rays".

> *"But for you who revere my name the sun of righteousness shall rise, with healing in its wings......"* (Malachi 4:2, NRSV).

Surely a sign of receiving our promise was in fact, the spring rain.

A Rhema Word

The week before the fourth altar-visit, I waited on God in prayer one afternoon. Though Saturday was usually the day of such visits, on Tuesday, May 24, I grabbed an hour and a spare room to be with God. Thinking about the signs we had already witnessed of heaven's affirmation along many steps of the way, once again my portion was listening, examining myself, asking God for His next step. Suddenly I was jolted powerfully out of the quietness with these words: *"There is the sound of abundance of rain!"* Like a bolt of electricity this Rhema word was a quickened and living conviction that started a root of faith in my heart. Though we had no idea about the physical state of the weather then (even in May it was very dry), the word left joy in my spirit.

Saturday, May 28 duly arrived and with Hannah, we set off for the next two altars of the Moon and Earth. The former no longer exists but on that site, out-of-bounds, is one of the nation's most powerful radio transmitters. We prayed several meters from the huge aerial, repenting and asking for a cleansing of the land. We entreated God to make a way for His Word to be beamed from here across the nation. Our three-way conversation with the Lord continued nearby, and when burdens had lifted we left for the next site.

Fourth Altar-visit

We bought tickets to enter the park where the Altar of Earth is situated and sat outside to pray. It had crept up unrecognised, but now a huge sense of tiredness suddenly overwhelmed me. Though I knew it isn't wise to go into spiritual warfare when one is so tired, the fact that June 12 was so close kept me from rescheduling this appointment. In fact there was no other time that I could think of! Hannah and I prayed together, asking for a fresh covering of the blood of Jesus, for renewed strength and protection and walked through the gate.

Altar of Earth Built in 1530, the site of this altar was an old temple dating from the Mongolian era (Kublai Khan's dynasty). During the Ming and Qing dynasties, it became the second largest of five temples in Beijing. The sacrificial ceremony bore similarity to that held at the Temple of Heaven. Before 1530 the two had been combined and called the Temple of Heaven and Earth. Since 1530, the emperor officiated at the Altar of Earth at the summer solstice dressed in yellow. Surrounded by a moat, the altar itself is a square shape, two terraces high — separated by a drop of six feet.[3]

Hannah and I approached from the west to discover all entry points closed except the south gate. As we curved around the outer walls of the altar I heard a little girl singing and paid special attention because I thought she had mentioned angels. I stopped to comment only to discover the song was *"Ten Little Indian Boys"!* Strangely it occurred to me that I was *meant* to think she was singing about angels, because this is what the Lord wanted me to know right now. I concluded indeed, that angels were going with us. Now at the entrance we bought another ticket, walked past the outer wall and began to pass the inner wall of the altar enclosure.

Immediately a very heavy atmosphere was apparent, and instinctively I turned my heart to praise the Lord with the first song that came. *"Through our God we shall do valiantly. It is He who will tread down our enemies. We'll sing and shout the victory. Christ is King!"*

Our passage through the only entrance seemed to confront the powers, for on the top terrace we discovered a curtained partition. It obscured the back of the altar from view but in the forefront on a green mat were positioned three people — two lying on their backs and one man in the middle. Catching our presence, the middle man began to move to a tight lotus position. Concentration became almost impossible. Hannah later told me she couldn't pray. Together we began to sing as loud as we could and though the sound of our voices cut the air like a knife, I didn't care.

So our walk around the altar began. As we rounded the corner, a frog croaked from somewhere down deep in the moat. Now the view behind the curtain revealed people in strange trances. One woman balanced a stick on one hand, another man balanced continuously on one foot. As we rounded the northwest corner a woman's eyes caught mine. She was seated, leaning over a child

---

3 Records tell us that at times human sacrifice occurred here. Robert Storey *Beijing City Guide* (Victoria, Australia, Lonely Planet Publications, 1996)p. 162

prostrate before her. It wasn't a pleasant expression, but it was the first eye contact we had made with this group. At the northeast corner another man on the lower terrace lay very still.

Our singing grew louder, and we slowly gained strength all the while continuing our circle, now round the south face past the entrance again. Shouting and making a noise, in English of course, gave us confidence for, apart from the sound of our voices, silence reigned. I pulled out my oil, the application of it being a symbolic invitation to the Holy Spirit to do His work in this place! On the pretense of tying my shoelaces, I began to anoint each corner of the altar. I didn't really know what to do next but prayed what came to mind and Hannah joined in agreement. We had to keep exalting and praising the Lord, but it was clear we were not to leave yet. It was kind of surprising what happened next.

From somewhere deep inside I either heard or remembered something because I began to laugh spontaneously. God was changing my thoughts — in fact consciously, I *knew* He was laughing now — I just laughed with Him. Then, the more I laughed the crazier it seemed, and the crazier it seemed the more I laughed. These people and their mind-concentration games were not a match for God! The more I laughed, the easier it became to think again. And then Hannah said, *"It sounds like the abundance of rain!"* She was referring to the sounds of laughter. I stopped in mid-tracks and said "*You've been reading my notes!*" Hannah didn't know that five days earlier on May 24, God had dropped those same words into my heart. In that moment it was obvious that a significant breakthrough had occurred. We both witnessed it.

Where there had been silence God had filled my mouth with laughter, as though to countersign what He was doing in the spiritual realm that day! As well, God had confirmed again there would be abundance of rain. We walked a few more times round the altar and then made our way unhindered, out of the enclosure.

The transformation was immediate. No longer tired, I was ready for anything! Jubilantly we said good-bye and each made our way home again.

Truly our experience that day matched these verses of scripture.

> *"He who sits in the heavens laughs: the Lord has them in derision [and in supreme contempt He mocks them]"* (Psalm 2:4, AMP). *"When the Lord turned again the captivity of Zion, we were like them that dream. Then was our mouth filled with laughter, and our tongue with singing: then said they among the heathen, the Lord hath done great things for them. The Lord has done great things for us, whereof we are glad"* (Psalm 126:1-3, KJV).

It was now two weeks before June 12, Sunday, May 29 and the occasion of the fifth group prayer meeting. (You will remember the fifth group prayer meeting was described in Chapter 3.) Hannah and I shared the testimony of the fourth altar-visit and the confirmed rhema word about *"abundance of rain"* with those present. Then it was our turn to listen in amazement.

On May 26, Deborah and Ruth were praying during their early morning appointments with God. The verse given to them was 1 Kings 18:44.

> *"At the seventh time he said, "Look, a little cloud no bigger than a person's hand is rising out of the sea." Then he [Elijah] said, "Go say to Ahab, 'Harness your chariot and go down before the rain stops you'"* (NRSV).

It also spoke of the coming of a huge deluge. Three times that week — on a Tuesday, Thursday and Saturday — the Lord had spoken independently to people in the group about abundant rain. This was the first, very strong message that there would be much precipitation in Beijing. To me, three such confirmations meant God was highlighting the message and emphasizing its importance. It had to have a literal meaning. In the week between the fifth and sixth group prayer meeting I decided to give serious attention to Elijah's story.

Elijah and His Prophecy — Abundance of Rain

Three years and six months after prophesying the drought Elijah was still standing alone, a voice crying against the idolatrous practices Israel had fallen into. Finally when the drought was severe and everybody was desperate, the message from God came to Elijah to present himself to King Ahab, that there would be rain on the earth. All of Israel would meet Elijah on Mt Carmel, including the prophets of Baal and Asherah. There would be a showdown on *their* mountain of worship. The confrontation was between Elijah and the idolators on one hand, God and Baal on the other. Baal may have been worshipped for many things but records mainly note him as god of weather, storm, thunder or lightning.[4]

When the prophets of Baal and company had had more than their fair share of time to hear from heaven, Elijah began to build the altar of the Lord. There was a special order to this; the altar had to be in accordance with God's pattern and will. As Elijah built the altar he was symbolically laying again foundation stones of faith in God.

Building God's Altars When we have pulled down the heathen altars we need to rebuild the altar of the Lord. His altars involve confession of sin, repentance, forgiveness and covenant renewal with God (see Genesis 12:7,8). The presence of the Lord did not

4 *Everyday Life in Bible Times* (The National Geographic Society, 1967)p. 90

fall at any altar just because it was an altar. Likewise, altars after God's pattern need to be built in our lives and cities before the presence of God comes, before the fire consumes the sacrifice. When the fire burns, we'll again yearn for Him with zealous verve, a revival fire of God that can't be stopped.

After the bullock pieces had been placed on the altar of sacrifice, Elijah ordered barrels and barrels of water to be poured on. What was he doing? Was he building an altar for himself? No. This deed done in obedience to the Lord was a symbolic preparation, an opening of the way for the Israelites to come back to the Lord. He was eliciting a response from them, calling them out of compromise to make a clean stand for God (1 Kings 18:21).

Elijah challenged the people to make a personal decision that either way would change everything. What was the issue? Very simply, worship. They had to choose which one was the true God and to worship him, but *not both*. King Ahab's idolatry had caused this curse of drought for over three years; now Elijah's question reminded them of the impossibility of serving two masters. Perhaps the debate was not whether they believed in God's existence but whether they *believed* His Lordship over other powers was supreme. Elijah's prayer was that God would reveal Himself to be Lord and God, so winning Israel back to Himself.

Standing in the Gap The process of re-building the Lord's altar in our region may involve a spiritual battle centering on worship. It will mean persistence and passion in worship, in the face of opposition. It will mean the confrontation of the lies and deceptions we have believed about God and ourselves. For example, fear is a lie against the truth of the Lordship of Jesus Christ and the everlasting love of the Father. Perfect love casts out all fear and Jesus is Lord everywhere. We *must not* be afraid to proclaim this! When the truth really hits home, wholehearted reactions are appropriate.

Back on Mt Carmel, Elijah's God answered with fire, showing the supremacy of His power and position. There was revival as the Israelites fell on their faces and shouted: *"The Lord indeed is God".* The display of God's power was undeniable evidence of the strongest One. The idolatrous tables were decidedly overturned by Elijah's God. Aspects for which Baal was worshipped — weather, storm, thunder, lightning — were the *very* things in which he was thoroughly humiliated. None then doubted the position of Elijah's God — Lord of the weather, and *so* Lord of the universe, King of kings and Lord of lords.

At the sixth group meeting on June 5, (the last before our Gideon Day on June 12) we made final plans for June 11, an indoors day of prayer. Also at this final gathering however, God had a battle for us to fight.

The Sixth Group Meeting

We usually began with worship, but today it was rough going. Though most had entered in, Deborah clearly picked up the urgency to worship. She began to exhort us over and over *"You've got to worship the Lord!"* The worship did crescendo until a measure of release came. Deborah was absolutely right. Finally, the significance of the notes God had given to share from Matthew 4, caught my focus! It was about Jesus' temptation in the wilderness. Now it was my turn to shout! *"I **will** worship the Lord my God and Him **only** will I serve."* Everybody joined in and again confessions grew stronger and louder. It was a struggle and our declarations became proactive, a statement of triumph in the face of God's enemy.

This spiritual battle was beginning to look a lot like Elijah's. It seemed to center around worship. The scriptures from Matthew 4:1-11 also teach us how Jesus won a strategic victory in a battle about worship.

How Jesus Overcame

Passing His forty day fast in the wilderness would have found Jesus at His weakest, humanly speaking. That's why knowing that He was filled with the Holy Spirit *before* the wilderness trip started was key (Luke 4:1). Though the tempter tried to ruse the Son of God into using His divine nature, He failed. Neither did Jesus pull a thousand power-packed punches against his opponent. He simply quoted scripture in the leading and power of the Holy Spirit and soundly defeated the devil. Jesus' obedience to the Father was high worship.

In my experience there have been many times when overcoming, as Jesus did in the power of the Holy Spirit, the Word of God and worship was the only way to obey God. *Regardless of the difficulty of our temptations obedience to God is paramount.* Jesus' victory, won as a human being only by the power of the Holy Spirit (not divine nature), opens the way for us to prevail in similar fashion. Certainly, advancing the Kingdom of God on earth will always mean displacement of God's enemy. We need to ask for frequent fillings of the Holy Spirit's power to do this.

Our declarations of worship had been confrontational in a spiritual sense, yet the Holy Spirit had led us through the sixth group meeting. The Word implores us to worship the Father in spirit and in truth (John 4:24) for it is part of our warfare. Matthew 4:9 tells us deceiving forces incited by the devil, seduce people into believing he is the god to be worshipped. Fighting deception was where the battle lay for us that day. It wasn't difficult to believe this meeting was critical in the Holy Spirit's purposes of prayer for the city. I didn't have time during this last very busy week before June 12 to research local issues more fully, but the big picture soon unfolded.

In China, as in other Asian nations, the dragon is worshipped. Though during the Cultural Revolution idol worship was substantially reduced, such images (and the phoenix, posed as his wife) have crept back to prominent visibility. Some places they are seen include National Day celebrations, national airlines, restaurants, decorative murals, historic places, fountains to name a few. Is the place this image takes in hearts of the nationals a high-profile one?

Chinese Associations — emperor/dragon/water

The Emperor was often associated with the dragon. Chinese historians though unclear as to the dragon's origin indicated it's evolution occurred over time from the days when people drew an animal and worshipped it. They would then surname themselves by the animal. Eventually the dragon became superior to all other animals, took on supernatural characteristics and subsequently became the ruler's emblem, then a symbol of the Chinese nation. Though only the emperor was permitted to use the dragon to represent himself, the Chinese to this day proudly name themselves descendants of the dragon. The emperor wore clothes embroidered with dragon figures and sat on a "dragon throne". He was acclaimed the "real dragon" and his descendants were hailed "sons and grandsons" of the dragon.[5]

The dragon, however, had it's own separate identity. The animal was credited as living in bodies of water for the purposes of protection and defense. Such abodes included rivers and lakes, mists and clouds along with their associates thunder, lightning and rain. The Chinese apparently believed in the need to appease the dragon to prevent devastation by floods and pestilence.[6]

Some highlighted the dragon symbol to reveal a link between

---

[5] Cheng Manchao, *The Origin of the Chinese Deities* (Beijing, Foreign Languages Press 1995) p. 71

[6] L.C. Arlington and William Lewisohn, *In Search of Old Peking* (Hong Kong, Oxford University Press 1935) p. 333

political power and **the role of water** in China's affairs.[7] It is not uncommon these days to hear contemporary political power being accredited with the ability to bring rain! Historically, this is traced to past emperors who began the practice of erecting altars to entreat the draco star for rain.[8] More belief in the dragon arose with the spread of Buddhism, and Taoism subsequently sided with this belief. By the time of Kublai Khan's reign in Beijing (or just before — notably the Northern Song Dynasty 960-1127), many dragon temples were built. The custom of praying to the dragon for rain became common and continues in some places today.[9]

Biblical Perspective The Bible is not caught unawares by cultural history. In His Word the omniscient Lord speaks of the dragon/water relationship and the dragon's death in the same verse.

> *"On that day the Lord with his cruel and great and strong sword will punish Leviathan the fleeing serpent, Leviathan the twisting serpent, and he will kill the dragon that is in the sea"* Isaiah 27:1 (NRSV).

The writhing, hiding character of the dragon-serpent along with its watery abode is uncovered in scripture simultaneous to the declaration of its death. Revelation 20:10 defines the final judgment awaiting the devil, also named the dragon or satan. As a created being the devil is not omnipresent, not omniscient, nor omnipo-

---

7 Madge Huntington, *A Traveller's Guide to Chinese History* (New York, Henry, Holt & Co.)

8 The draco star is reference to the Pole Star, which over the centuries has changed constellations. The Pole Star 4620 years ago was Thuban, brightest star of the constallation 'Draco' or Dragon. Thuban is no longer the Pole Star. Read the interesting story of how the Pole Star is now part of a constellation telling of Christ's birth in the book by William Banks *The Heavens Declare* (Kirkwood, MO, Impact Books, 1985) p.78 The title of the Forbidden City in Chinese is "Purple Forbidden City", purple being a reference to the color the Chinese have given to the Pole Star. This was an implication that the emperor was the central body around which everything on earth turned. Consequently, the northsouth axis of the Forbidden City was centred around the Pole Star. Roderick Farquhar and the Editors of the Newsweek Book Division, *The Forbidden City [China's Ancient Capital]*, (Published by Newsweek Book Division, 1972) p. 72

9 In 1998 postcards were being sold of people entreating this god for rain around altars.

tent. Neither is he supernatural, nor can he create rain! Instead he delegates power to varying levels of wicked spirits with the purpose of seducing people to believe that he can do these things (See Ephesians 6:12, 2 Timothy 2:25,26). In this way people have welcomed the lie of idolatry in China.

Worship Issues

Themes about worship of the one true God, (in spirit and in truth) have been discussed throughout this chapter. For greater and continued breakthroughs pure Holy-Spirit led worship will always be a key. In this way our personal decisions for light or darkness do impact families and generations to come.

Everyone of us faces worship issues. Worship is what fascinates, captivates and changes us, both negatively (to ensnare us away from God) and positively (to draw us closer to God). For intimate worship we must fall in love with God, order our lifestyles aright, and be obedient as well as become flexible in the ways we worship. The abandonment to passionate worship means learning what pleases the Lord. To be truly in love with Him means to express that adoration, in prostrate surrender, hushed awe, harmonious song, deliberate confession, loud shouts of praise, dance, or contagious laughter. Worship is dying to our own ways and our own wishes lest we create a god of our own desiring and so fall into idolatry.

It's a costly road, but shouldn't it be? The nature of relationship is reciprocal. Jesus came to save us from destroying ourselves, from the mutilation of our bodies and the pleasing of angry so-called gods. Instead, He brought good-will to the human race and began to make His former enemies into His friends. He invites us to receive His love, the welcome of the Father, His full acceptance, intimacy and glory. No less! It's no wonder that a response to the Almighty requires wholeheartedness and undivided love. Worship *is* an acknowledgement by all that we are of Who He is. It's adoration of the surpassing beauty reflected in every aspect of His nature. He loves us to spend time with Him. He is Love; we can safely let Him take over.

God used Elijah to teach us about worship. Just as He did with the Gideon story, God began to use 1 Kings 18 to draw out parallels with the prayer for Beijing. Elijah's story was just the assurance I needed to know we were on course. What an awesome God He is! On June 5 we didn't yet know the facts that unfolded about Chinese culture. Neither had we made the connection that this chapter suggests; that similar to Baal in Elijah's time, the dragon in Chinese history had been worshipped as the god of rain. The altar-visits had been completed, curses broken and along the way God had told us clearly of the abundance of rain to come. There was even a special invitation for an evening of worship hosted by independent musicians from the International Fellowship. We were excited about the timing of that event after our sixth group meeting. As I think back on the way that happened without our intentional organising of it I am amazed.

The Holy Spirit's leading and the Father's faithfulness were so evident in this intensely busy period. Frankly, it was hearing from God through the power of the Holy Spirit, the prayer of team members and intercessors from home, and commitment to the Lord that kept it all together. And then, still others heard from God about rain that week preceding our Gideon Day!

PRAYER POINTS:

• That altars of repentance, forgiveness and covenant renewal would be built to the name of the Lord. *'And the Holy Spirit testifies to us, for after saying, "This is the covenant that I will make with them after those days, says the Lord; I will put my laws in their hearts, and I will write them on their minds," he also adds "I will remember their sins and their lawless deeds no more." Where there is forgiveness of these, there is no longer any offering for sin'* (Hebrews 10:15-17, NRSV).

• That the millions of Beijing would know, *"The Lord, He is God, the one and only true God, besides whom there is none else"* 1 Kings 18:39 (KJV). *"Hear, O Israel: The Lord is our God, the LORD alone. You shall love the LORD your God with all your heart, and with all your soul, and with all your might"* (Deuteronomy 6:4,5 NRSV).

• That the church would bear fruit in keeping with repentance and live in God's love to give it away. *"Bear fruit worthy of repentance"* (Matthew 3:8, NRSV). *"Love has been perfected among us in this: that we may have boldness on the day of judgment, because as he is, so are we in this world. There is no fear in love, but perfect love casts out fear; for fear has to do with punishment, and whoever fears has not reached perfection in love. We love because he first loved us* (1 John 4:17-19, NRSV).

CHAPTER FIVE

The 'Gideon Day'

'When Gideon heard the telling of the dream and its interpretation, he ***worshipped****; and he returned to the camp of Israel, and said,*
"Get up, for the Lord has given the army into your hand"'
(Judges 7:15, NRSV), (Emphasis added).

On Saturday June 11, 40 people gathered together indoors for prayer. Firstly we shared the encouraging signs that God had given us during the week. Steven spoke about his dream of a storm followed by peaceful rain. When he'd finished somebody else interjected they had had exactly the same dream. And there was another report to tell.

Once a week over the past several months I had been meeting with Priscilla and her special team of intercessors. I would share with them particular needs and messages the Lord had given me. In turn, they upheld us all in prayer. Now, in the final week before June 12, Priscilla had some news. In the course of his duty as an embassy official, her husband had been present at a meeting with a high-ranking general of the Chinese army. At some point the general had commented that it would rain in Beijing on either the 9th, 10th or 11th of June.

Hearing Priscilla talk that Tuesday about the Chinese general's prediction of rain sent me scurrying to prayer, asking what this was all about. Could a sign from the enemy's camp be trusted? We already knew that *much* rain was coming. What did this new message mean for us in the prayer strategy, if anything? I was in the middle of my question to the Lord, when the recollection of Gideon's sign stopped me short.

Gideon's sign 'from the enemy camp'

In the evening of the day that the selection of the 300 soldiers was completed the Lord said to Gideon:

> *"Get up, attack the camp; for I have given it into your hand. But if you fear to attack, go down to the camp with your servant Purah: and you shall hear what they say, and afterward your hands shall be strengthened to attack the camp"* (Judges 7:9-11a, NRSV), (Emphasis added).

That day Gideon's little band of 300 had just been pulled together. They were hopelessly outnumbered but the Lord's instructions to Gideon for attack came the same night! (There was no time to develop Plan B in case everything went wrong!) Gideon's obedience must have been essential to the Lord (and precious), because He arranged some encouragement. An enemy soldier had a dream and this, along with the dream's interpretation was told to his fellow. Gideon heard it all with his own ears. Think of it! The prophecy of Gideon's future victory was spoken by his enemy. *No wonder* Gideon and his company were strengthened to attack. *No wonder* Gideon responded in worship.

When I saw the *purpose* of Gideon receiving this sign from the enemy camp — to strengthen for the attack — I was encouraged, too. In fact deeply moved would be a better description of my feelings. What a remarkable way God was choosing to strengthen us! It was a final message to say *"You're in correct position for the battle ahead!"* Especially realizing the similarity it bore to Gideon's story for us *the night before* our *Gideon Day* left me speechless.

Our sign

The rain did come — on the night of June 11 — and that the rain was a sign from the Lord was confirmed. When they awoke the next morning Rebekah and Deborah received identical scriptures about rain which they later shared with us:

> *'God setteth the solitary in families: he bringeth out those which are bound with chains: but* ***the rebellious dwell in a dry land****. O God, when thou wentest forth before thy people, when thou didst* ***march through the wilderness****; Selah. The earth shook,* ***the heavens also dropped at the presence of God****: even Sinai itself was moved at the presence of God, the God of Israel. Thou O God didst* ***send a plentiful rain****, whereby thou didst* ***confirm thine inheritance****, when it was weary'* (Psalm 68:6-9, KJV), (Emphasis added).

The scriptures speak for themselves, and give a perfect description of the Father's 'going out before us' using the rain to affirm His little band of pray-ers in Beijing. It was hard to fathom all the wonderful messages from Heaven for there seemed to be no end to His faithfulness.

In telling this exciting part of the story I've jumped ahead to June 12! We began the chapter with June 11 — let's go back for a brief summary of that day of indoor prayer.

June 11 — Warfare Prayer

On four poster sheets we had written the names of strongmen perceived to have a hold in the city. Just before we went to warfare prayer there was once more repentance and prayer for national sins in case any had been missed. The spontaneous prayer we shared at the end of these group times could be summed up as follows:

> *"Father, in Jesus' name we entreat your forgiveness for our sins which have given invitation to these powers to take hold in the city. These sins include abdication of our wills and leading others to destruction — we have so courted control, war and death. Forgive us that we have not wholly abandoned ourselves to You O God, the author of life. We have worshipped other gods in detestable ways and so given them licence to deceive and control us. Forgive us where we have not listened to your servants, O God, for we have allowed lust and control to drive us and block our hearing. Forgive us that we have believed lies about You, O God, and engaged in idolatry. Shame and confusion have come to us and our kings and princes and to our people because we have sinned against You. In prideful and arrogant ways we have built walls to keep You out of our city and our lives. We do not present our prayers to You according to our own right ways, but because of Your great mercies and lovingkindnesses. O Lord, forgive! O Lord, heal and cleanse, set our city free! O Lord, this is Your city and Your people who are called by Your name!"* (This prayer was taken from Daniel 9).

After this petition flowed specific prayer to the Lord Jesus that the strongmen of war, the dragon, the "ne zha" entity and divination (witchcraft) would be pulled down. There were spontaneous shouts and great declarations of God's victory. The four posters at the front of the room now became the focus at which our scriptures were hurled! By this stage we had written verses such as these on the blackboard:

> *"Let the high praises of God be in their mouth, and a two-edged sword in their hand; to execute vengeance upon the heathen, and punishments upon the people; To bind their kings with chains, and their nobles with fetters of iron; To execute upon them the judgment written: this honor have all his saints. Praise ye the Lord"* (Psalm 149:6-9, KJV).

We were graphically expressing the victory of Jesus over these strongmen when suddenly Joshua's inspiration to put the posters on the floor released our faith in a new way. We began to stomp all over those poster cards. As if by signal prayer participants marched around the room in a circle allowing each person the opportunity to pound the posters. I sensed faith rising in me and judging by the sound of the shouts this was true of others also. And then something else emerged, for as we marched together, there was one moment when the voices and stomps melted into one. We would talk about it later — the moment the breakthrough in the heavens had come.

Quite a session of prayer and praise was about to come to an end when I detected the descending of God's presence. *Again,* it was the restraining hand of God *causing* us to be still and wait, to sense Him communing with us Spirit-to-spirit. How can one express the presence of God adequately? I can only say He took my breath away. Aware that it was lunchtime, I waited for some minutes and finding myself at a loss for words simply asked the Father to establish our morning's prayer according to His will.

The afternoon resumed on other prayer topics for our city. Once more we broke into small groups to remember the government before God. Finally, there was the allocation to prayer teams of sites they would visit on June 12. To do so each prayer team was invited to pray and ask the Lord which sites He wanted them to visit. Each team received their instructions quickly, and were confident that they had heard from the Lord. There were particular characteristics and logistics about each place that made the matching job of sites with teams a complex one. For example some places required more prayer than others, but whatever the story, the Holy Spirit did a perfect job of administering each assignment. Within 20 minutes every group had their site allocation and associated research profiles.

We parted company on Saturday afternoon with final instructions. Team leaders were to bring elements (bread and grape juice, or the next best available) in preparation to hold communion at many of the prayer sites. Secondly, oil was to be provided for teams to use also. (Invitation of the Holy Spirit's ministry was to be made by prayer and the symbolic application of oil.) There were rumbles of excitement as teams discussed finer details. The Gideon Day, June 12, was here at last!

The Gideon Day — Praying on the Streets

Following the rainfall of the night before we awoke to a beautiful day. It was perfect for our job of praying at sites; with plenty of people around enjoying the weather, we could easily blend into the crowd. A total of 34 city locations were visited. (Please see Appendix D for details). We were amazed at the favour we received at many locations to venture unhindered into areas usually banned entry to the public. I have chosen to share four testimonies of answers to on-site prayer.

- **Tiananmen (Tower Gate):** This tower gate or rostrum flanks the northern side of the Square, separated from the Square by

Changan Street. The tower itself is ten meters high and includes a decorated rostrum accessible by stairs to the top. This rostrum was of great importance to the city and empire in ancient times — the place where edicts were issued, the ruler of the empire was crowned, and married. Heaven's rule has been identified with this gate (and the dragon throne) for over 800 years. The gate's name means heavenly peace and harmony although the reality especially during the last century has not reflected this.

Abigail and Michal proceeded up the stairs to the Rostrum. At the top, Michal felt compelled to stamp her foot *as if* she had a stone in her shoe. She kept stamping until the strong feeling had gone. Having already discovered there was no stone in her shoe Michal interpreted this impulse as originating from the Holy Spirit. It could indeed have been a leading of the Spirit of God, in keeping with this scripture:

> *'Thou shalt tread upon the lion and the adder: the young lion* ***and the dragon shalt thou trample under foot'*** (Psalm 91:13, KJV), (Emphasis added).

Anna and Esther prayed at street level around the rostrum tower, or Tiananmen Gate. They welcomed the Lord Jesus and prayed that the real peace of heaven would reign here. We know these two areas have been prayed over many, many times by Chinese and foreigners alike — and God is still leading individuals and groups in prayer for His will to be done here. One day the scales will tip for God's Word to be proclaimed and His name to be exalted appropriately, in one of the most honored places of the nation. Until then we pray and obey.

> *'Lift up your heads, O you gates; yes, lift them up, you age-abiding doors, that the King of glory may come in. Who is*

[He then], this King of glory? The Lord of Hosts, He is the King of glory..'(Psalm 24:9-10, AMP).

• **Altar of Land and Grain** (Zhongshan Park): This was the altar described at the beginning of Chapter 4 where the Emperor traditionally made sacrifices to the gods of the earth and five grains. It was built in 1421, the floor covered with five different soil colors representing five basic grains. This altar also distinguished for the Chinese the four cardinal points of the compass, with China as the centre of the universe in the middle. China means *middle* country, identifying for the Chinese their independence and integrity.[1]

Mary and Esther had first visited this altar back on April 9, feeling led of the Holy Spirit to circle the altar seven times and speaking release of souls for salvation to the north, south, east and west. Again on June 12, Esther arrived with a team who set themselves to pray for the lifting of a heavy atmosphere. Firstly, communion was held where sacrifices had been offered. Along with thanks for what Jesus had already done for us on the cross and for His cleansing, prayer was made that the strongman over the altar be bound. Immediately following the communion feast and prayer, everyone noticed that the atmosphere had lightened considerably. Esther happened to look up in time to see the blackest, darkest bird flying away from the altar towards the south. The others also witnessed it's departure at the prayer-time's end; this was interpreted as a sign of God's answer and His work to bring spiritual liberty here. In fact, the change was so evident Esther couldn't help but sing!

Surrounding the northern, central and southern lakes of central Beijing many places of significance are situated; we divided this

---

1 L.C. Arlington and William Lewisohn, *In Search of Old Beijing* (Hong Kong, Oxford University Press, 1935, 1987) p. 71

large place, the stomach, into A and B.

• **Beihai Park, Qiongdao (Island) and Northern lake : Part A** Located on the island, and the northern lake's shoreline are a number of Tibetan buddhist temples. The image of the city god of Beijing is set there.[2]

The prayer team that stopped at this site on June 12 was the same as the research team. They knew that a difference in the spiritual atmosphere had taken place, a displacement which was further established when prayer and communion was offered on that Sunday. They accredited the change to the power of God and His Word, in answer to their prayer.

• **Zhongnanhai (Central and Southern Lakes): Part B** The western shoreline of these lakes is primarily occupied by the residential government compound while the Forbidden City flanks the eastern shoreline. The lakes and surroundings were originally part of the Imperial Palace enclosure and this place once doubled as a royal resort. Until 1911, governments carried out their reigns from within the Forbidden City. Once the emperors' palace, this once "forbidden city" is now open to the public. The left side of the Forbidden City and the western shoreline however are completely inaccessible to the public, flanking as they do, current government headquarters.

Joshua's team met at a spot on the western wall of the residential compound and split in two. Each half of the team then circled the northern and southern walls respectively, meeting mid-way on the eastern wall of the compound. They prayed about the the area adjacent to the western walls of the Forbidden City, the present government headquarters, which had also

---

[2] This idol image is different from the "ne zha" image. Such idols, also called "city gods" were traditionally put in place to watch over cities. They were usually of an evil appearance for the purpose of frightening the city dwellers into obedience. Cheng Manchao, *The Origins of the Chinese Deities* (Beijing, Foreign Languages Press, 1995), see the chapter on city gods.

become a "forbidden city". They asked the Lord to break the spiritual connection between the two gates of the Forbidden city and Zhongnanhai compound. Their walk concluded with communion, song and spontaneous shouts of victory. A scripture verse was read aloud:

> *'And at the seventh time, when the priests had blown the trumpets, Joshua said to the people, "Shout! For the Lord has given you the city.."'* (Joshua 6:16, NRSV).

• **Gulou** (Drum and Bell Towers); The apex of the northsouth axis is located here.[3] During Mongolian rule this was taken as the geometric centre of the city; the placement of the outer city walls was determined from this point. They were also time keepers until 1924. Drum rolls tolled the hour watches and the copper bell rang out the hour at seven every morning. From Yong Lo's time (1421) the geometric centre was moved south to the man-made "Coal Hill."

Joshua's team anointed tower gates and doors and the bell in the Bell Tower. Communion was held and a song of victory was sung after a time in the Bell Tower. At the top of the Drum Tower, with a view overlooking the city, prayer was made briefly for each of the city's suburbs. Suddenly a loud obvious disturbance of the swallows at the moment petitions began caused quite a commotion. It was taken as a sign of God's timely intervention in the city in answer to prayer.

Team Briefing

At 3:30 P.M. when all the teams arrived at the debriefing ren-

---

[3] See Appendix D and note that a line runs from north to south. This has occult significance. It originally started at the drum tower in the north and continued all the way to the Temple of Heaven in the south.

dezvous, the jubilant sharing began. The Lord's work among us had been confirmed often with signs.

A Good Report: The Lord's protection of us all was complete. Chinese attendants and service personnel were courteous and helpful. For example, Priscilla's team visited the Great Hall of the People (where the National People's Congress is held) and participants were given permission to enter rooms not normally open to the public. This team was also granted access to the innermost of sanctuaries in two old catholic churches where they prayed, held communion and anointed many places.

At another temple site a team member prayed for healing for one of the temple goers who then went home peacefully. In the centre of a busy intersection where once an east city gate was located, another team sang praises openly to King Jesus, welcoming Him to the gate. They sang to the accompaniment of a guitar and no one stopped them!

That Sunday afternoon Michal reported a vision she had received the day before. She recorded it as part of her testimony of God's faithfulness:

> *"I'm really thrilled and excited to be a part of all this. I had a word from the Lord the week before June 11 and 12. I had been getting in my quiet times a picture of a torch. I didn't quite understand what this torch meant. On Saturday as we were singing, 'Shine, Jesus, Shine, Fill [Beijing] with the Father's glory the Lord showed me a picture [which you see at the opening of the Olympic Games, of the huge bowl and the runner carrying the torch.] When you dip the torch into the bowl it blazes forth and you set the whole thing on fire. He was showing me that we were like His torch. As we went out to the city sites so His light was going to blaze forth in those places."*

It had been a very intense weekend, but now was a time for refreshment and renewal — and that's what happened as we began to worship the Lord. His presence again fell in a very evident way and some said they had never experienced such a time in their whole lives! Others were full of thanks for being able to participate. We praised God for His lovingkindness to us in a strong city!

Redemptive Gift: In the last moments of the meeting the Lord prompted me *twice* to mention the redemptive gift of Beijing, or His purpose and destiny for the city. He intends Beijing to be a place for national and international meeting together, for peace-filled, upbuilding and profitable communication. Like Jerusalem, God loves Beijing deeply.

People wanted to share so many testimonies that Sunday afternoon that another meeting was scheduled for the next Saturday, June 18. Among those stories was one about six members from a Chinese basketball team who unexpectedly gave their lives to Jesus all at once that same weekend of June 12. Other participants noticed an increased interest in the things of God from local friends immediately following June 12. That Saturday, team members also shared personal testimonies of the dealings of God in their lives over the months of prayer for Beijing. One was Rachel.

> *"When we were walking around the government compound, the 'new Forbidden City' next to the old one, I wasn't afraid. [Despite] all the trouble we've been through in China I didn't feel afraid. My main concern was how to get to the wall and anoint it. I've struggled [in the past] with seeing police and shuddering. I just know now that the fear is gone. It is the grace of God.*
>
> *I was reading a book by C. Peter Wagner about snares you can fall into when you're doing spiritual warfare in the city. One of the things [he said] was to recognize the power satan*

has and not to get puffed up in your pride, but not to be afraid at the same time. That's what I'd been experiencing this whole time. [There was] the respect that satan is an awesome power and the [humility] that we so desperately need Jesus' power because we don't have it [ourselves].

As we get ready to leave China I praise God because I see things differently from when I first came. I'm not afraid of communism anymore. The fear is totally gone. I thank God, because I think this involvement that Jacob and I have had in this [prayer strategy] has sealed this in my heart. I thank God that He has helped me deal with this kind of fear."

God's work in individuals is as important as what He did in the city, though I cannot fully measure all that He did in either sphere. The faith of many grew and there was fulfillment of God's promise of protection and unity;[4] also many signs of God's presence and answers to prayer which I have already noted. We worked with much diversity among participants. Often English was a second or third language, and differences shared included cultural, vocational and church backgrounds! We glorify God for all He began and that He will complete.

What of the abundant rain God had so clearly promised? That was our question, too! On June 11 and 12 rain fell as a sign to encourage us before our Gideon Day. This was not the fulfillment of God's promise to us. In our hearts we all felt the same, that the story was not over. Then we heard news of the drought.

PRAYER POINTS:

- That Beijing will become a place for national and international reconciliation, and peaceful, upbuilding communication.

---

[4] A history of division in the Body of Christ in Beijing dates to the sixteenth century — see footnote 11, Chapter 2.

"All this is from God, who reconciled us to Himself through Christ, and has given us the ministry of reconciliation; that is, in Christ God was reconciling the world to Himself, not counting their trespasses against them, and entrusting the message of reconciliation to us. So we are ambassadors for Christ since God is making his appeal through us; ...." (2 Corinthians 5:18-20a, NRSV).

• That the jealous, zealous love of God would become a message of unmistakable clarity to Beijingers. *'Between the vestibule and the altar let the priests, the ministers of the Lord weep. Let them say,"Spare your people, O LORD, and do not make your heritage a mockery, a byword among the nations. Why should it be said among the peoples, 'Where is their God?'" Then the LORD became jealous for his land, and had pity on his people'* (Joel 2:17,18, NRSV).

CHAPTER SIX

Abundance of Rain

*"And it came to pass in the meanwhile that the heaven was black with clouds and wind, and **there was a great rain"*** 1 Kings 18:45 a-b (NRSV), (Emphasis added).

The next day, Sunday, June 19, Miriam informed me of news she had heard. When she randomly turned on the radio to Voice of America a few days earlier the next item reported that Beijing, China was in the grip of its worst drought in 94 years. Everybody was being told to conserve water. It's not unusal to be out-of-touch with local news in China, but we had also been very busy and had failed to notice articles such as this in the China Daily on June 15, 1994:

> *"A widespread summer drought will likely affect this summer's harvest of winter wheat in the North and seriously affect other crops in the south. There have only been 10 millimeters of precipitation since Mid-May or 60 to 70 percent less than average rainfall in North China, officials for the State Anti-Drought Office (SADO) said yesterday.."* June 3,

> 1994. *"A senior expert yesterday related that the current 18 month drought is the worst of the century. The capital city is rapidly reaching water scarcity and facing limits to further economic development due to the persistent spell of dry weather,.." Teng has resorted to shock-therapy in trying to get city residents to understand the depths of the drought..'*

On Friday, June 24, the eve of the Marches for Jesus around the world it rained most of the night in Beijing. We felt the rain was in answer to intercessory prayer from other countries, and this added strength to our convictions. God's promise of abundant rain was making more and more sense! Like Elijah who stayed on his knees waiting for the cloud to appear and then grow bigger, we stayed in prayer, reminding God of His promise. Now we *needed* a miracle!

An Age-old Problem

A miracle comes at the height of desperation. According to the newspaper articles, the desperation could have been understated. In fact as I look back now, the lack of water in Beijing was a repeated theme during our months of prayer. Remember the professor at the beginning of Chapter One? This man with the heart of a city father was the first to alert us to the fact. He said that no matter how *much* water was channeled from afar, regardless of the population count, there had never been enough.

The professor's statement was confirmed in the climatic history. Remember the Chinese proverb that expressed the value of spring rain? *Spring rain is as precious as oil.* Again, the legends confirmed it. I will paraphrase part of one to highlight the ground condition.

> Before any cities were built, the plain [on which Beijing is built] was called *Bitter Sea*. The people had to live in the western and northern hills, while the dragon king

> lived in the *Bitter Sea.* The dragon king and his wife, son, daughter-in-law and grandchildren controlled the *Bitter Sea,* so that all the people lived a very miserable life.. The dragon king and his wife were captured,..... After the capture, the water *slowly leaked away..* The name of the plain was changed to *Bitter Sea Waste* (Italics added for emphasis).[1]

Again, legends are not true to life, but they may support what the Holy Spirit says about local beliefs or bondage of the land.

What had God been saying to us about the water situation? Two scriptures were given to us around this time:

> *"He turns rivers into a wilderness, water springs into a thirsty ground. A fruitful land into barren, salt waste* ***because of the wickedness*** *of those who dwell in it"* (Psalm 107:33,34, AMP), (Emphasis added).

Other scriptures the Lord gave us on the eve of our Gideon Day from Psalm 68 also expressly referred to Beijing's water situation. (Especially see Psalm 68:6-8; The Amplified Bible says ...***the rebellious dwell in a parched land*****).** Last, but not least, was the *confirmed* promise that God would bring us abundance of rain. Now there was a serious drought. It was time for God's move!

We had prayed about many of these things as the Holy Spirit led us, but it appeared still more intercession was needed. Now confidence, a rest within and certainty settled on us that God would come through, but I would not have guessed His next directions!

---

[1] No author listed, *Sights with Stories in Old Beijing (*Beijing, Panda Books, Chinese Literature Press, 1990) pp174-180; Jin Shoushen, *Beijing Legends* (Biejing, Panda Books, 1982) pp 10-17.

The Story Continues

On Sunday, June 19, as I went home with news of the drought somewhere in the back of my mind, another word interrupted my thoughts. Out of nowhere the word "llama" popped up and then a memory from my childhood of the animal that spits. I prayed about the memory and gave it to the Lord. However later that day, finding myself unable to concentrate, I seriously told the Lord, in *no uncertain terms* about the weariness and pressure I felt at the end of the hectic term. He seemed to be trying to get my attention and I asked for lots of confirmation! The vague sense that God *was* speaking persisted, and on June 20 I mentioned the issue to Him again! My comprehension of His request was to do a prayer visit to the Lama Temple. From even a historical perspective this was the strongest hold of Tibetan Buddhism within China outside of Tibet. I told God that this was not combat any battle-weary soldiers should engage in!

A Mountain

On the Monday night of June 20, I woke in the midst of a dream involving spiritual warfare with a Lama priest. After more prayer I went back to sleep and dreamt of a huge mountain. It was a formidable mountain, steep and difficult to climb, without any trees on its slopes. The sides of the mountain consisted of gravel. The slopes looked deceptively easy to traverse but I knew that anyone who tried to climb would be unable to, encountering danger if he tried. On top of the mountain was a pyramid-shaped steel cap; strong and impenetrable. It glistened proudly in the sun. As I took in this view, I was suddenly standing at the lowest point below the mountain directly in line with the top. Surprisingly, an immense joy grew within so that I became certain of conquering the mountain. My confidence was such that I felt certain nothing could stand in the way to the top.

This second dream was a reminder (in God's language) of the grave danger involved if we tried to fight in our own strength. But at the same time, the Holy Spirit had imparted His joy and courage during the dream. God would give us this mountain!

The next morning I willingly told the Lord that I would obey Him and take a prayer team to visit the Lama Temple. I also asked Him what day we should do this. He immediately said, July the 2nd. About to open my mouth in protest that an unavoidable appointment was scheduled for that day, I thought better of it. By mid-morning the institution informed us of the re-scheduling of events on July 2nd. The day was free! Hardly believing my ears and in complete awe of God, I broached the subject with friends formerly involved in the Gideon Day strategy.

How did they respond? Some replied that this had already been on their hearts. They were waiting for me (Esther) to hear from God! Others not normally enthusiastic about spiritual warfare requested a prayer visit to this site. Scriptures about mountains were being given to these people. One person even awoke around 3 A.M., unable to sleep and started researching the Lama Temple! There seemed to be quite a sense of relief among team participants that we should go ahead. This willingness could only have been the moving of the Spirit of God. After our intense three months' prayer strategy and days before the end of term, this co-operation was a mark of true humility!

The Big Picture

In fact, I had one and a half days free before July 2nd to begin research on this topic. As usual, my questions began with the big picture. If there was a reason for the problem, there must be a root. Information was difficult to find, but a number of points unfolded that proved to be key.

The worship of Tibetan Buddhism consists of many incantations and much chanting and unmentionable pagan practices. The formation of the sect came from an ancient Bonn Tibetan group that practiced occultic rites and worshipped the *thunderbolt.* A thought began to develop in my mind. In Gideon's time, Baal was worshipped for thunder, lightning, the storm. Weather was the very aspect through which his humiliation came, in the form of rain. I wondered if, by reason of pagan worship rites, a curse had similarly been placed on the land.

Exposing Evil, Though Not Condeming People At this juncture, especially because of the story that follows, I want to assert that any facts presented are not intended to arouse curiosity about demonic activity. Neither do I intend to incite condemnation of those who historically incited evil deeds, but simply to expose the devices of the enemy so that God's people can walk in all the liberty that Jesus Christ purchased for us. In fact, whether Buddhist priests or Moslem ayatollahs', shamen or witchdoctors from darkest Africa, all these are people created by God in His image. Recently unbelieving Moslem ayatollahs have received direct revelations from God which led them to Christ. In short, it is the truth we have heard often: *love the sinner but hate the sin.* Though the sin *should repel us,* we must be careful not to pass judgment on sinners. The most hopeless of all sinners can be transformed by God's power. While there is breath there is hope!

Let me give you a case in point. History has recorded that Ghengis Khan was one of the most savage and ambitious (I've heard it said *the most ambitious*) conqueror this world has ever known. How is it, then, that Kublai Khan his son had more than a passing interest in Christianity? Consider this.

On Demand by Kublai Khan

The Tibetan Buddhist presence became established in Beijing from the time of Kublai Khan, but once during his reign Kublai

Khan questioned their practices.

In fact, there were Christians in the populace. While not a Christian, the Mongolian Emperor showed great favor towards them. He must have had a curiosity about Christianity though, to request such a large number of qualified Christians from the Roman Pope. Italian visitors to his court, Matthew and Nickolas noticed his interest and asked him why he didn't embrace Christianity. He replied (in part);

> *"If I become a convert to the faith of Christ and profess myself a Christian, the nobles of my court and other persons who do not incline to that religion will ask me what caused me to receive baptism and embrace Christianity. 'What extraordinary powers,' they will say, 'What miracles have been displayed by its ministers?...'"* [2]

The emperor was referring to the magicians and sorcerers of his court who exhibited power even to the extent of holding back bad weather. He was respectfully careful not to antagonise them, though he had the authority to put them right as the Emperor. He was bound to give his allegiance to the powers *revealed* as supreme, and in that regard his world view was defined by his experience.

I believe it was an honest question the Emperor asked, for not all miraculous power comes from God (see Exodus 7:11-16). Moses and Aaron were not intimidated by Pharaoh's magicians, when their demonic power turned rods to serpents. God's servants stood their ground and His superior power was revealed when Aaron threw his rod on the floor, which turned to a serpent and devoured the others.

---

[2] Edited and with an introduction by Milton Rugoff, *The Travels of Marco Polo* (Copyright, The New American Library of World Literature Inc., 1961) p. 125

It was the omnipotence of the Almighty God that clearly demonstrated Who was the Lord of hosts in Moses' day. Pre-eminence of the strongest is a law of the universe set by the transcendant God of all. He is no stranger to challenges, for the Bible tells many stories where He is Victor. What a great Warrior God is!

The problem with Kublai Khan and officials of his time, was that although recognizing the power of the spirit world as real, they didn't know it was destructive. Perhaps many would chose differently if they witnessed the unequalled power of God *and that He is the most kind and merciful of all.* Biblical Christians do not deny the reality of God's adversary, nor of the devil's schemes, tricks and power. On the contrary, we know our worship is appropriate for the all-powerful, all-knowing, ever-present supreme God. As we exalt Him, the devil's henchmen are bound and his accusations and lies are silenced. The Father graciously chooses to display His transcendent power and glory in the face of opposition that the lost and hopeless may find redemption. And He is still making a great name for Himself in this way today.

It's possible that "greater works" would have helped Kublai Khan believe in Jesus as Lord. Though he had no experience or knowledge of the Almighty, he wisely left his options open as seen from the job description of the 100 Christians whom he invited to teach his court.

> *"They were to be qualified to prove to the learned of his dominions by just and fair argument that the faith professed by Christians is superior to, and founded upon more evident truth than any other; that the gods of the Tartars and the idols worshipped in their houses are only evil spirits,and that they and the people of the East in general were under an error in revering them as divinities.*[3]

A valid and precisely put requisition, it was a plea for Christians to show him witness of the true God. A follow-up promise was that if His supremacy could be proved, all nobles and subjects of the court including himself, would be baptised. It is one of the saddest indictments of Christianity that no Christian teachers ever responded to the invitation during his lifetime. Marco Polo commented:

> *"From this it must be evident that if the Pope had sent out persons duly qualified to preach the gospel, the Great Khan would have embraced Christianity, for it is certain that he had a strong leaning towards it.*[4]

According to historical records the opportunity offered Christians was not taken. By default another door was opened for divination and the occult. In fact, history tells us that Kublai Khan became a devout Buddhist.[5]

Let me ask this question: *"I wonder who will be held responsible on judgment day for his decision to turn away from Christ?"* Since none of us really knows all the facts, I can't say for sure. My point is that we be careful to avoid a "better than they" attitude, and a self-righteous, condemning view. We *must* walk in grace. Remembering that Jesus came not to pass sentence on or reject the lost, my petition is that in judgment the Most High God would have mercy on all of us.

By this time we had repented for the failure of Christians to take up Kublai Khan's invitation (see the end of Chapter Two). We dealt with the original sin but we needed to do spiritual warfare to take back lost ground. Then, it became clearer why God's next instructions led us to the temple.

---

[3] Ibid., p. 39
[4] Ibid., p. 127
[5] L. C. Arlington and William Lewisohn, *In Search of Old Peking* (Hong Kong Oxford University Press 1935, 1987) p. 207

Friday July 1st — Indoor Prayer

On Friday afternoon about twenty-five people gathered for prayer. Once more we began with worship. In a corporate prayer we renounced all incantations and curses from the occult level and freshly submitted ourselves to the Lordship of Jesus Christ. (To my knowledge everyone present was convinced of God's will for their personal involvement in this prayer strategy.)

The research we had been able to gather was perused, after which the group broke into smaller groups to repent before the Lord for sins of idolatry and divination associated with this temple.[6] Repentance brought some "clearing of the air" but, persisting in prayer, we began loud declarations of scriptures the Lord had given us about mountains. These were two:

> *"Behold, I am against thee, O destroying mountain, saith the Lord, which destroyest all the earth: and I will stretch out mine hand upon thee and roll thee down from the rocks and will make thee a burnt mountain. And they shall not take of thee a stone for a corner, nor a stone for foundations; but thou shalt be desolate for ever, saith the Lord"* Jeremiah 51:25,26 (KJV).

> *"Is not my word like a fire [that consumes all that cannot endure the test]? says the Lord; and like a hammer that breaks in pieces the rock [of most stubborn resistance]?"* Jeremiah 23:29 (AMP)

---

[6] This included magical and sexual rights, works of sorcery, animal and possible human sacrifice, violence and witchcraft. Judith S. Levey, *The New Columbia Encyclopaedia* (New York, London, Columbia University Press, 1975) p. 2745, 2691
Some tour guide books recommended caution as people were known to have completely disappeared at the site. L. C. Arlington and William Lewisohn, *In Search of Old Peking* (Hong Kong, Oxford University Press, 1935, 1987) p. 195

In keeping with these were other scriptures from Isaiah 41:15 and 49:2, which confirmed that our warfare was to be in the form of declarations. In agreement with the written Word of God we spoke to the mountain before us. Suddenly Deborah stood up and began another loud declaration:

> *"There is something effectual happening here today and you will not speak lies to our minds, you will not bring confusion and you will not stop us from praying!"*

There was hearty agreement and a breaking of the confusion; it became easier to think, pray and speak. Others quickly followed in the speaking out of other scriptures pertaining to the Lord's hatred of magic, sorcery, witchcraft, violence and lies. One verse was repeated over and over, and interestingly it seemed to bear reference to both the physical and spiritual situation of the city.

> *"Shower, O heavens, from above, and let the skies* ***rain down righteousness****; let the earth open* ***that salvation may spring up****, and let it cause* ***righteousness*** *to sprout up also: I the Lord have created it"* Isaiah 45:8 (NRSV), (Emphasis added).

Soon after these declarations it occurred to me to make the following command: *"To the drought condition in north China: come into Divine order, now!"* Quite a bold order that was — but I can tell you I felt pretty insignificant saying it. This was the first time any such prayer had been uttered in our meetings.

We had prayed every way the Lord had indicated, but the battle was far from over. Spiritual warfare had already been heavy and tomorrow would be a big day. We concluded the meeting and I encouraged everyone to remain in prayer.

Prayer Visit on site — Lama Temple — Saturday, July 2nd

Three interceded for the team at home while twelve pray-ers met on-site. Comments made as people arrived were indicative of the intensity of the battle. Prayer was made for those feeling sick. Then we grouped into two teams of six and then began the walk. From our northern location, each team walked around one side of the temple towards the southern end to the only entrance.

We had prepared to hold communion and made the suggestion that those willing should kneel on the street as a sign of submission to the Lord Jesus. Bowing down in public was not something we had done a lot of in this particular city. Now it was to be done as a sign of humility in contrast to the pride in our surroundings. There was a powerful release of the mercy of God as we did so. Suddenly it became very easy to thank God for the gift of salvation, for the privilege of knowing Him and of being kept by His power. We prayed joyfully, in thanks to the Lord of glory for leading us to pray at the particular location that day! Amazingly, none of the passers-by in the vicinity of either teams paid us the slightest attention.

The two prayer teams now at the entrance prepared to go forward, asking for a fresh covering of the blood of Jesus and His protection. Joshua spoke of an inspiration from the Holy Spirit to buy a miniature Buddha; his intention being the later smashing of it inside the temple. Joshua took leave to purchase the object and immediately another member of Joshua's team approached me. He had independently received the same idea from the Holy Spirit. Those two did smash their buddhist figurines in faith that it would precede Jesus' toppling of this site. Their simple obedience to the Holy Spirit honored and agreed with the instructions from the Third Person of the Trinity! His idea had been witnessed by two — we can be certain that in the end, God's plans will not be thwarted!

Esther's team continued with declarative prayer using scripture through the walk to the northern section of the enclosure. The Holy Spirit led us to the large idolatrous image where we proclaimed the Word of God and a huge oil mark (a sign of our agreement with the Holy Spirit's work) was left on the base. Communion was held at the temple altar area where we simply repented for the shedding of innocent blood and thanked God for what He wanted to do there. At 11:40 am I looked at my watch and began the walk south, out to the main gate. Just ahead was Joshua's team. We heard later that at 11:40 am precisely, our prayer support team ceased their intercession.

Cleansing Prayer We prayed and cleansed ourselves immediately upon arrival outside the south gate. We specifically renounced any incantations spoken over our lives and freshly anointed ourselves with oil, while pleading for a fresh cleansing of the blood of Jesus. These prayers are vital at such a time. Upholding the cross of Christ between us and any who have spoken curses will put an end to the matter. We also took time to anoint each other's feet with oil and asked for a strengthening of our individual walks with the Lord Jesus. Then we caught taxis back to the meeting point.

Abundant Peace

It was easy to share testimonies before entering into worship. Quite unnoticed at first, the Presence of God descended among us. We came to an end of our songs. There was unusual peace, abundant rest and quiet. It was not to be interrupted. Each one received according to their need, but I like to think it was Love come down. Somebody even said; *"It was like God was giving me a hug!"* The word given us from the Lord was that He was replenishing His workers. That wonderful Presence of God lasted for half an hour and then *reluctantly*, we went home.

Abundance of Rain — Sunday July 3rd

At the dawning of the morning we awoke to a wet, sodden city. Rain, glorious rain! I don't know why I knew this was *'it'!* Leaves, twigs, stones and bushes were awash with water and everything else seemed alive with clean air.

There was indeed, something different about this rain, something so peaceful and right as though it was full of life and blessing. Not driven rain, making one run from the storm or heavily filling one with fear and encumbrance. This rain was like a clean pure sense of refreshing life. It seemed that as the rain continued, the city was being washed cleaner and cleaner. Perhaps it's no wonder, considering that God answers prayer. We had prayed this verse:

> *"Shower, O heavens, from above, and let the skies* ***rain down righteousness****; let the earth open* ***that salvation may spring up****, and let it cause* ***righteousness to sprout up also****: I the Lord have created it"* (Isaiah 45:8, NRSV), (Emphasis added).

Of course, in saying that the rain was "like a clean sense of refreshing life", I am referring to a spiritual aspect. As the Bible verse indicates, I believe this rain was doing something physical and spiritual; cleansing, for example, can be both.

That Sunday morning we freely uttered ecstatic thanks to Almighty God for the rain. He had kept His word, the promise of abundant rain. Joyful shouts and embraces were the order of that day, and others didn't mind in the least canceling their planned open air activities.

The rain did prove to be heavy and bountiful, yet several of us commented to each other on the pattern of its fall. The timing of each downpour seemed to follow an order, as though responding to signals from another Source. It rained all day Sunday and most of Monday. However there was no rain Monday night or part of Tuesday. Tuesday night and all day Wednesday brought heavy rain. Thursday there was no rain but on Friday and Saturday it rained heavily. There seemed a purpose to this pattern; perhaps to give the earth a chance to soak up each installment of this "precious oil". The pattern continued in like manner as long as the rain fell, for all of July and half of August. There was more evidence of answers to our payers for the city, too.

The Drought Broken — Friday July 15

About two weeks later on July 15, 1994, an article was published in the English Edition of the China Daily, stating that the drought had broken. It read:

> *"Two days of torrential rains this week ended Beijing's worst drought this century... The downpour which began Tuesday and lasted for 30 hours, enabled the city's only source of fresh water, the Miyun Reservoir, to store more than 300 million cubic metres of rainwater, the largest amount in recent years ...."*

I remember being caught in that rain! It was a joke trying to stay dry so I just gave in and enjoyed it. There was so much of it! Campuses were deluged with water and roads were often flooded, since the city drainage system was apparently unable to handle the volumes of water. God reminded me again of Gideon and his band of 300, which is the Biblical number of deliverance. 300 million cubic metres of rainwater (and more) is a sure deliverance from drought!

Much later, at the end of August, a friend handed me another newspaper article. It reported that on July 15 (the same day as the publication above) at 1:00 P.M. in another drought stricken city of north China a temple collapsed in the rain. Published by a Hong Kong paper, The Eastern Express, parts of this article are quoted here.

> ***Rain Slays 'Dragon' of a Thousand Years***
>
> *'Traditionalists view the crumbling of an imperial palace in Henan province as a portent of political change, reports Bruce Gilley. A thousand year old imperial palace — a portent symbol of the autocratic power of China's rulers — collapsed into a heap of mud and tiles last week, prompting speculation as to whether the catastrophe portends political change. Worn flagstones and heavy rains were blamed for loosening the foundations of the Dragon Pavilion in Kaifeng, Henan province, which came crashing down at about 1:00 P.M. Raised on an ox-blood colored foundation towering over down-town Kaifeng, the corbel and bracket roofed pavilion was the imperial palace of the Northern Song dynasty (960-1127) ..... "...Kaifeng represents a sense of history and continuity to the central government", said a member of the culture, education and science committee of the National People's Congress (NPC)'.*

Kaifeng is a city located 600 kilometres due west of Beijing. I certainly remembered that my prayer had been for the drought condition over the whole of north China to come into divine order. There sure was plenty of rain everywhere in the north, apparently. However, I did ask the Lord if there was any other significance to this event that He wanted us to note. As the newspaper article hinted, there was a historical background to this story. The Lord led me to dingy libraries and out-of-the-way places once more.

Pertinent History

You will remember how Kublai Khan began the process of conquering China in 1126AD. Two dynasties were toppled, the Northern Song Dynasty which ruled the west, and the Qin which ruled the whole of the north east with their capital 20 kms southwest of present day Beijing. (Recall that this was the city burned by fire called Chengdu, but not to be confused with the Sichuan provincial capital of the same name.)

The Mongolians firstly conquered the Northern Song Dynasty. Their imperial headquarters were in the Dragon Pavillion in Kaifeng. As I discovered, this Pavillion was quite famous at the time, considered a great structural model so that other temples were fashioned after it. That was the age when in Kaifeng and throughout China many entreated the dragon for rain.[7] The imperial palace in Kaifeng therefore, once a seat of government and dedicated to the Chinese god of rain, was none other than the Dragon Pavillion which collapsed in the rain on July 15, 1994.

The second dynasty which Kublai Khan overturned was the Qin, and the first thing he did was to level the imperial palace in Chengdu or City of Swallows. This palace was also carefully modeled and constructed after the Pavillion in Kaifeng.[8] It would seem there was more than a passing connection made in Beijing with this Pavillion in Kaifeng, at least in the Chinese mind. The newspaper claimed a historical connection or *"continuity"* between

---

[7] Cheng Manchao, *The Origin of the Chinese Deities* (Beijing, Foreign Languages Press, 1995) p. 71

[8] To the Chinese of that day it was essential to have as exact a replica of the Kaifeng Pavillion as possible, for they went to painstaking ends to copy it, even conveying many building materials from Kaifeng to Beijing. Zhou Shachen, *Beijing Old and New* (Beijing, China, New World Press, 1984, 1985) pp. 15,16

Kaifeng and central government. As implied previously, the Chinese attribute spiritual and cultural power to the governmental body and its representatives. I believe that as this deified symbol of power from the past came crashing to the ground, God was making a name for Himself.

PRAYER POINTS

• That God's righteousness would continue to be rained down in these times, causing righteousness and salvation to sprout up in Beijing. We pray: *"Shower, O heavens, from above, and let the skies rain down righteousness; let the earth open, that salvation may spring up, and let it cause righteousness to sprout up also; I the Lord have created it"* (Isaiah 45:8, NRSV).

• That mountains against the Lord would be levelled and valleys would be lifted up in preparation for the full revelation of God's glory. *'A voice cries out "In the wilderness prepare the way of the LORD, make straight in the desert a highway for our God. Every valley shall be lifted up and every mountain and hill be made low; the uneven ground shall become level, and the rough places a plain. Then the glory of the LORD shall be revealed, and all people shall see it together, for the mouth of the LORD has spoken"* (Isaiah 40:3-5, NRSV). *"I will go before you and level the mountains, I will break in pieces the doors of bronze and cut through the bars of iron"* (Isaiah 45:2, NRSV).

PART TWO

CHAPTER SEVEN

Broken Covenants

"The land and the earth mourn and wither, the world languishes and withers, the high ones of the people [and the heavens with the earth] languish.

The land and the earth also are defiled under their inhabitants; because they have ***transgressed the laws****, disgregarded the statutes,* ***broken the everlasting covenant****"*
(Isaiah 24:4,5, AMP), (Emphasis added).

The story of this book which culminated in Chapter 6 was about the abundance of rain, a chronicle concerned with healing of the land. It had certainly been withering under severe drought and the seasonal cycle of rain had stopped. The scripture says the earth and land are *under* the inhabitants of the earth who have defiled it. Another example of this by way of testimony is appropriate here.

It was my first walk across the intersection but already quite a reaction was registering inside. There was defilement in the air. Uncleanness, hatred, even sexual debasement were reflected in the surroundings, too. Though I have rarely felt unsafe in China, I would try never to be in this area after dark. As well, everything was dirty, especially the roadside vegetable and meat markets just off the corner. Every building that lined the corners had that "old, it's-not-worth-cleaning-me-up" look about it. There were often traffic jams. It was usual to see small crowds of people observing two in the midst of an argument. When I drove through the same place with others, they reacted in a similar way. Although my workplace for three years was located in the vicinity of that intersection, I avoided it like the plague.

The puzzle remained unsolved for two years, when a local friend 'Small Willow' and I prayed to ask the Holy Spirit for the cleansing of our compound. A few days later 'Small Willow' happened to be in conversation with an old man who had been a gatekeeper for many years. As 'Small Willow' later told me, the retired gatekeeper volunteered much information about our workplace *and the intersection.* He said that around 1935, a truck load of Japanese soldiers was traversing the intersection when it crashed and collided with apparatus on the roadside. Most of the soldiers died on impact or were wounded fatally. A few days later 'Small Willow' and I went to the intersection to pray cleansing for the intersection. We repented for the shedding of innocent blood and broke curses over the land, later returning under the cover of darkness to hold communion, again asking God to heal and cleanse the area.

I wish you could see the intersection now! It wasn't until two and a half years later that I had an opportunity to return to the scene. Actually, I had forgotten the matter until passing by recently, but then I was suddenly surprised by the change and remembered our prayer for the cleansing of the land there. On the corner near where the truck had crashed the land has been cleared and a new supermarket is now open for business. It even *looks* clean. Up and down the road the street is swept and clean. Traffic lights have been installed. Just up from the west-side, a new building has been built to house the former open-air market. Now painted, it is enclosed and tidy, even clean. I did see one crowd of people, but there was a lack of animosity in their voices as though they were trying to help each other solve a problem. No longer is there defilement in the air and for the first time I felt safe. In a real way, I felt one of God's purposes for my time in the area had been accomplished.

Healing of the Land In 2 Chronicles 7:14 the healing of the land was dependent on God's people humbling themselves, seeking His precepts, His face and turning from their sin. In the above testimony, the shedding of innocent blood (whether by accident or intention was unclear, but this) had polluted and cursed the land and its people around the intersection. We repented for the sin (which affected *us* and our environment) and the change was wrought in prayer.

Upon becoming aware that a particular location is defiled we will need to ask the Holy Spirit to make known to us what has happened in the past. In my experience He is pretty quick at availing us with what we need to know. Bloodshed is not the only way land is defiled as we will soon see from the scriptures. However until we ask, and until there is repentance and cleansing of guilt, our world bears the consequences at least to the fourth generation.

Defilement of the Land Though the cause of defilement has been forgotten, the people buried and the records burnt (as regularly happened in China), the record of sin and defilement remains before God. God gave the land of Caanan as an inheritance to the Israelites and their generations. The brevity of their individual lifespans meant they were to be caretaker-tenants, with the Lord as Landowner. We too are transients, temporary residents (Leviticus 25:23, 1 Chronicles 29:15), and are likewise required to account for the trusteeship of our land to God. It is an ongoing responsibility. Issues of defilement from past eras must be dealt with if we are to see the Landowner Himself pour out unmitigated blessing.

Ineffective wardship of the land can prevent God's purposes from being realised by its people. The land bears the consequences of ungodly management (Deuteronomy 21:1-9; Numbers 35:33). Especially where the undeserving have died, the land cries out (see Genesis 4:10,11), and bears the curses from violation of God's laws. Living in a cursed land doesn't help anybody! Our job is to buy back the land's fallen trusteeship to accountability and productivity in God's ways.

It is true that prayer for a nation covers many aspects. This book is a call to prayer and repentance for the people of China and their land. Many scriptures such as Leviticus 27, Deuteronomy 28 and of course 2 Chronicles 7:14 mention the land and its people together. In the recognition of the land's defilement, God is giving us a key to repentance for the people and their unconfessed sin. In step with the Holy Spirit Whose job is to uncover sin, we can bring healing. It is important to ask specific forgiveness for the wrong done, *and* to purge (by asking in prayer that the blood of Jesus, also *cleanse*) the guilt of the innocent. In this way the sin is forgiven, the punishment pardoned and the land is freed (Isaiah 59:1-16). Through Jesus, our Redeemer, we appropriate His redemption.

Defilement of the People If the curse of historical sins affects the land, then it impacts present-day residents, too. When sin is unrepented of it will remain to plague future occupants of the land though they have never wilfully participated in the original sin. Our communities, families, churches and cities become fettered with bondages while wounds and sins from the past are reproduced. The land writhes and its people languish under violation, abuse and spiritual contamination because, as it says in Isaiah 24:4,5, they have *transgressed the laws, disregarded the statues, broken the everlasting covenant.*

These phrases — the laws, the statutes, the everlasting covenant — reveal the relationship between individual actions, what others do to us and how our forefathers have passed sin on to us. They teach us the impact of sin, and the land's defilement on future generations. Our purpose now is understanding how defilement occurs. We can then repent and redeem the land for God.

What are the laws of God?

The Ten Commandments are the laws which God gave to the Israelites to teach them how to live in His ways. They teach us the four major ways that the land is defiled; idolatory, bloodshed, broken covenants and immorality. These laws (see Exodus 20:3 to 17) can be divided into four major sections and we will look at them briefly. Firstly consider:

Our relationship with God: (Exodus 20:3 to 7). Exodus 20:3 says:

> *"You shall have no other gods before or besides me"* (AMP).

To worship God means He is in the first place in our hearts, homes and lifestyles. This requires an undivided heart of love and service to Him alone. When we put other gods in the Almighty's rightful place, we incur iniquity on our lives and on future generations (Deuteronomy 20:5, Isaiah 42:11). In Exodus 20:4 and 5 (see also Deuteronomy 5:8,9) we are told of the consequences:

> *"You shall not bow down yourself to them or serve them; for I the Lord your God am a jealous God, visiting the iniquity of the fathers upon the children to the third and fourth generation of those who hate Me, But showing mercy and steadfast love to a thousand generations of those who love Me and keep My commandments"* (AMP). *"And first I will repay double for their iniquity and their sin, because they have*

> *defiled My land; they have filled My inheritance with the carcasses of their detestable and abominable idols"* Jeremiah 16:8 (NKJV).

Defilement# 1: Idolatry brings a curse, a defilement of the land. To be free of it will mean repentance for worshipping anyone or anything other than God. We must turn from worship of our own creation rather than the Creator.

The day of rest (Exodus 20:8-11) is a profoundly simple ordinance but the Holy Spirit led Moses to write four verses of explanation. Our bodies need it but we are instructed also to dedicate this day to the Lord. Once we have turned our lives over to God, our bodies are the temple of the Holy Spirit so taking this rest is a form of worship. To the Israelites God said:

> *"'You shall keep the Sabbath, therefore, for it is holy to you. Everyone who profanes it shall surely be put to death; for whoever does any work on it, that person shall be cut off from among his people. 'Work shall be done for six days, but the seventh is the Sabbath of rest, holy to the Lord. Whoever does any work on the Sabbath day, he shall surely be put to death'"* Numbers 31:14,15 (NKJV).

From my own experience I can say the lack of rest is something that leads directly to our becoming task-oriented rather than people-oriented. It causes us to see people as parts of a schedule and things we have to do rather than those with whom we need to share the Father's love. We become "cut off" emotionally. We then walk into control, we build walls, and "me" tends to always be in charge. In a land where control is a major cultural trait, this is a form of defilement!

Defilement #1 — Idolatry (Continued) Violation of the sabbath of rest as a law of God is another form of idolatry. It leads to exclusiveness, an independance that could eventually lead us away from the Body of Christ. Rest and recreation are pivotal to health and happiness individually and corporately. Repentance of this sin will cause us to find new delight in God and to be fed with the good inheritance of our eternal heavenly Father (Isaiah 58:13,14).

Honoring our fathers and mothers (Exodus 20:12) is a powerful and vital emphasis we must have if there is to be well-being in every area of our lives. This is the first commandment with a promise. If we give respect to and regard our parents in a godly way, life will be long and go well. If, on the other hand, our parents were relationally immature or unhealed from life's hurts, then we may find it difficult to honor them. This usually leads to our judgment of them and the promise may be lost. In Deuteronomy 5:16 God said again:

> *"'Honor your father and your mother, as the Lord your God has commanded you, that your days may be long, and that it may be well with you in the land which the Lord your God is giving you'"* (NKJV).

Defilement #2: Broken Covenants Promises made to us that were broken or that we made to others that were broken are a cause of defilement. We need to repent for judging and dishonoring our parents, lying and compromising, then forgive and let go of the pain of others' broken promises and betrayal to us. We need to repent for the ways we have defiled others by not keeping our word. To be really thorough, we may need to pray about issues at personal, family, church, community, city and national levels.

From the beginning of our lifetime parental relationships significantly impact so much of our lives for good or otherwise. The following commandments deal with God's relational laws. They are placed after the command to honour our parents because breaching of these laws grows out of unforgiveness towards our parents. If we can completely forgive those two primary people with whom we have related from the beginning of our lives then the seeds of rebellion in other areas will be washed away. The roots of hatred will have no soil in which to grow.

Do not murder (Exodus 20:13) is a straightforward commandment. Paul wrote in Romans 13:8 and 9 that fulfilling all the law could be summed up in the second commandment. Leviticus 19:17 and 18 puts it so well:

> *"'You shall not hate your brother in your heart. You shall surely rebuke your neighbor, and not bear sin because of him. You shall not take vengeance, nor bear any grudge against the children of your people, but you shall love your neighbor as yourself: I am the Lord'"* (NKJV).

Defilement #3: Bloodshed defiles as it involves murder, manipulating events to cause the sacrifice of others' lives and taking vengeance against other people. The shedding of blood pollutes the land (Numbers 35:33,34) especially when against innocent people. Intercessional repentance here would require dealing with all forms murder (even suicide and war), hatred, grudges, anger, jealousy, bitterness, rage, criticisim, lies and judgments retained against others.

Do not commit adultery (No immorality) (Exodus 20:14) is a commandment that is widely violated in modern times and has been, down through history. What a wonderful thing that we can repent for our sin and the sin of our ancestors, for violating this commandment, or any of the law, brings defilement.

> *"For whoever shall keep the whole law, and yet stumble in one point, he is guilty of all... So speak and so do as those*

who will be judged by the law of liberty" (James12:10,12, NKJV).

Defilement #4: Immorality is a violation that brings defilement to the land (Jeremiah 3:9). In Ezekiel 16:25-27 the imagery of ritual prostitution was a picture that emphasized the gravity of Israel's idolatry. Sexual immorality is often a form of idolatry (spiritual adultery) against the Lord. As the Amplified Bible says in verse 26, they had *".. multiplied their [idolatry and spiritual] harlotry."* The Israelites lost their "food allowance" and were delivered to their enemies because their lifestyle did not reflect God's Lordship. Pornography, prostitution, adultery and homosexuality are all causes of defilement, a door that opens up great wickedness to the land (Leviticus 19:29). The cities of Sodom and Gomorrah, given over to homosexuality were destroyed from the face of the earth by *"vengeance of eternal fire"* (Jude 7, NKJV). These are things we need to take seriously by repenting. Otherwise the church of Jesus Christ will lose authority and take on a lust for power and authority (control), losing its servant heart and all traces of humility.

The Ten Commandments not only tell us how our sin defiles the land and other people. The consequences of breaking God's law teach us the importance of our repentance toward God. They also tell us about God's everlasting love. A significant portion of God's communication with Israel was in the language of covenant. He wanted to teach them and us how to incur blessing.

What is The Everlasting Covenant ?

God first made a covenant with Abram in Genesis 15. The patriarch gathered three animals and two birds and prepared them as a sacrifice. This was part of the covenant-making process. When darkness fell, the Lord spoke. He mentioned a land Abram and his descendants would possess. Two chapters later in Genesis 17 the

Lord appeared to him again and outlined an everlasting covenant. It would be between God and Abraham and his descendants for ever. The covenant was fixed by a solemn pledge (*oath*) between them. The land of Canaan was to be the everlasting possession to the Israelites and their descendants. *The exchange of possession* was to indicate handover of God's dominion to man, a display of complete trust and support. (They effectively became caretakers of the land on God's behalf.) As a *sign of the covenant* Abram and all the males of his household (and later his descendants) were to cut their flesh in the circumcision act. It was to be a reminder to the people that they belonged to Him. When the Israelites were leaving Egypt, they were to place the blood on the lintels and posts of their doors so the death angel would pass over their families. At that time they shared the passover meal, a *sealing* of God's covenant with them. Whenever the covenant was violated, an animal sacrificed by the violater would effect substitution on his behalf, to restore atonement with God.

Interestingly, as God gave each word of the Ten Commandments to Moses, the fire of God actually *cut the stone.* Though the Israelites had never seen God, this "cutting of Covenant" was a sign they would have read and believed as for real! The commandments were the Covenant parameters that set up conditions for either blessing or cursing.

Ramifications of the Everlasting Covenant could be one of two kinds. If the Israelites obeyed the laws and kept within its parameters, the Everlasting Covenant would bring much blessing. Because it was made with Abraham and his descendants, the laws concerned every individual and every one of the 12 tribes of Israel, literally the whole nation.

If they kept the conditions their offspring would be blessed, along with the produce of the *ground,* their herds of cattle and flocks. Deuteronomy 28:11 sums it up:

> *"And the Lord will grant you plenty of goods, in the fruit of your body, in the increase of your livestock, and in the produce of your ground, in the land of which the Lord swore to your fathers to give you"* (NKJV).

God's blessings were reflected on the *land*, too. From Him the rain would come to the land in due season, and all the works of His people would prosper. God Himself, the First representative of the Covenant, would also be blessed by the Israelites obedience. All the peoples of the earth, would have a holy respect for God's people. Why? They would see the way His people were blessed above others, and be drawn to the one true God. God would make a name for Himself! What a powerful form of evangelism!

If they disobeyed the laws there would be consequences. The curses would affect the 12 tribes and later the nation. Disobedience would bring curses on the corporate nation though sin was committed individually. Remember Achan (Joshua 7:10-13)? There would be:

- No increase on the land and no fruit (Leviticus 26:20)!
- The heavens would stop the rain, and there would be no pasture for the cattle; the cattle would die (Deuteronomy 11:17, 28; Joel 1:1-18).
- The land would be brought to desolation (Leviticus 26:32).
- Famine on the land; crops would fail or be destroyed (Psalm 105:16).
- Drought on the land, mountains, harvest, men, cattle, and man's labour (Haggai 1:11)!
- Defeat for God's people who would now run from their enemies seven ways (Deuteronomy 28:25)!

- Consequences of lost dominion; trouble on the land was not immediately removed (Exodus 23:29).
- Cursing, confusion and rebuke on everything God's people set their hands to do (Deuteronomy 28:20).
- Fatal diseases and filth on the land and its people (Ezra 9:11, Deuteronomy 28:22).

All of God's blessing — His bounty, love, provision, protection, beauty, justice, judgment and life — is exhibited on the land. The land reflects God's character, for it belongs to Him. He cares for and shields it (Psalm 47). He wants to bless it and our work in the field and city (Deuteronomy 11:10-12, 28:12). Therefore, when the ground is cursed because of sin the earth mourns. As it continues to mourn and suffer violation, it affects the inhabitants. Romans 8:22 says that all creation groans and travails in pain. Isaiah 24:6 says that the curse has devoured the earth. We must take notice of what is happening to the land. It is an object lesson, a wake-up call to take up right trusteeship of the land!

The Everlasting Covenant stated there was a curse to the fourth generation, on God's people who left Him for other gods. Not only was the earth defiled until the sin was repented of, but sin became generational.

What is Generational Sin?

The Scriptures speak repeatedly about sin being carried over to other generations. We have seen some of those consequences already. Let's look at Numbers 4:18 to remind ourselves of what the scripture says.

> *"The Lord is longsuffering and slow to anger, and abundant in mercy and lovingkindness, forgiving iniquity and transgression; but He will by no means clear the guilty, visiting*

the iniquity of the fathers upon the children, upon the third and fourth generation" (AMP).

The law of generational sin was originally the law of generational blessing, set in place by the Father Who intended that the universe would build itself up in love. Blessings would be multiplied generation by generation (to a thousand generations) of those who loved God and obeyed His laws. Then sin entered the universe and the same law meant to bring blessing now brought cursing. The sins of the fathers then began to assail their children to the third and fourth generation.

The general problem of sin was addressed very early on in Genesis 3:15, when God spoke of His promise to bring a deliverer who would deal with the devourer. This One is Jesus who died on the cross and rose again that we could surely be forgiven and receive eternal life. He bore the price of our sin and its punishment.

Let's look at that. Amazingly, it's all in the language of Covenant.

The New Covenant

The new covenant *in Jesus blood* was just that. Under covenant terms, the agreement was made through Jesus' blood, by our covenant representative, Jesus. In the following steps, note the italicized words, which highlight the covenant terms.

Step 1 Long before the world was created, the *site of sacrifice* (Calvary) and the *covenant representative* (Jesus) were chosen by God. Amazingly, He is the lamb slain from the creation of the world! (Revelation 13:8).

Step 2 Jesus became the *sacrificial lamb* used in the covenant ceremony. He was split open with the spear, blood and water gushed out, His body was broken.

Step 3 Before He died Jesus invited His disciples to the Passover meal. Giving thanks for the bread Jesus outlined *His oath: "'Take, eat: this is My body, which is broken for you: do this in remembrance of Me." In the same manner He also took the cup after supper, saying, "This cup is the new covenant in My blood. This do, as often as you drink it, in remembrance of Me." For as often as you eat this bread, and drink this cup, you proclaim the Lord's death till He comes'* 1 Corinthians 11:24b-26 (NKJV).

Step 4 Jesus' *garment was sold (exchange of possession)* to a soldier. As our covenant representative He identified with our nakedness, shame, humiliation and sin. The giving of His garment afforded His intimate identification with us.

Step 5 The scars on Jesus' hands, feet and side are *signs of the covenant* that remain in His body forever! Jesus' life was no longer His own. Those signs on His body, signs of our victory, are forever recognisable by friend or foe (John 20:27)!

Step 6 *A new name* is reserved in Heaven for those who overcome (Revelation 3:12).

Step 7 Before his death, Jesus invited His disciples to share the *Passover meal.* This feast, also called the communion feast, was the *sealing* of the new covenant.

In celebrating the communion feast, we are proclaiming the death of Jesus. It was His powerful blood which ratified the New Covenant. In thanking Jesus for giving His precious blood, we uphold and proclaim the significance of the covenant, so honoring the unbreakable union we have with God. Through Jesus' spotless blood we have forgiveness, cleansing, freedom and life. In His death Jesus took our weaknesses and exchanged them for His strength. We take on all that is His, healing, authority, power, destiny, love, grace, bounty and much more. It is all ours *if* we *appropriate* the blood by faith in prayer. God has made His children covenant-partakers both individually and corporately but we need to take up our side of the covenant and own our inheritance.

Salvation and Generational Sin

A question arises about salvation bringing forgiveness from our sin. Though born again, how is it that we still need to repent for sins of past generations? Why do we still need to apply the blood of Jesus?How is it that we need to deal with violated laws of the Old Covenant and defilement of the land, since we are under the New Covenant? Positionally we are delivered from the power of sin to entangle, but every Christian will testify to the fact that experientially we still sin. This is despite being radically born again. Also, every Christian will have seen some of the signs of defilement of the land. The answer, I believe, lies in understanding that Jesus (through the New Covenant) did not come to do away with the law, but rather to fulfill it (Galatians 3:17).

What about the law? When Jesus died as our covenant representative, the devil was judged as a murderer and a liar from the beginning. He was declared defeated, condemned, at the cross. 1 John 3:8 says Jesus came to undo, (the Amplified says destroy, loosen and dissolve) the works the devil has done. Through the cross the devil now has no way to pull us down except where we have been taken down — through our own sins. However, the devil has no power over us when we plead the blood of Jesus and our covenant rights over them. In response to what the law says, we need to know the terms of the New Covenant, that Jesus is now the eternal sacrifice for our sins. We are justified by the blood of Jesus, not by obeying the law (Romans 6:14, Galatians 2:16, 5:6.) Do we need to heed the law, then? The law shows us where we have come short of God's standard.

The Law and Repentance Paul also wrote that the law was given after the promise to disclose and expose to men their guilt (Galatians 3:19). It implies that we are responsible to deal with our sin, personal and generational. God still requires repentance of us even after salvation.

Are we included in the Everlasting Covenant today? The scars on Jesus' body were signs that will remain on His body for ever — the covenant is everlasting! As we have seen, God will one day give us a new name which will be ours forever, and this is also a sign of the Everlasting Covenant. Remember the Old and New Testament Covenant rights? We partake in the blessings of the Everlasting Covenant God made with Abram through Jesus Christ. The law could not cancel the promise. (Galatians 3:14-18).

Waging warfare In the New Testament the principles of the Ten Commandments were not annulled, but rather upheld (Romans 3:31, 8:4; 13:8). If the law was not done away with, then the curses of disobedience can be incurred, too. Through our faith in Christ we will have to repent, apply the blood of Jesus and wage warfare over issues relinquished to the devil's hand by our forefathers for those generational curses to be broken. This can be done for our own personal history. Often in the process we can repent for the defilement of the land and do warfare for societal and national breaking of generational curses.

Applying the Blood It is with confidence we can apply the blood to weak areas of our lives for cleansing, protection from attacks, deliverance and strengthening in God's grace. Even as the Israelites pled the blood of the animal over the lintels and posts so the death angel would pass over their homes, we can apply the blood of Jesus to our homes, our possessions and our lands. We have been given tenancy of them. As we come under the Lordship of Jesus Christ and under the New and Everlasting Covenant, so do they. God expects us to take care of His possessions and His land and pray for unredeemed people who are also part of His creation. We are to do good, taking care of the land under the terms of the Everlasting Covenant, to reap increase and liberty in creation. This, I believe, is what Romans 8:19-21 speaks of:

"For the earnest expectation of the creation eagerly waits for

> *the revealing of the sons of God. For the creation was subjected to futility, not willingly, but because of Him who subjected it in hope; because the creation itself also will be delivered from the bondage of corruption into the glorious liberty of the children of God"* (NKJV).

We have been entrusted with so much under the terms of the Everlasting Covenant, and it does include a priestly wardship of creation and the land. God has assigned us dominion over the work of His hands (Psalm 8). The above scripture speaks of the maturation of God's children preceding the liberation of creation. What an exciting time is ahead!

Confession of sin Despite the groaning of creation, God desires that none would perish and all would have their hearts changed in repentance (2 Peter 3:9). God loves people more than anything. As we pray for our cities and nations we are touching a subject very close to the Father's heart. Whether interceding for healing of the land or its people, it is good to remember that in both Old and New Testaments, the process of getting things right with God, or repentance, involved confession of sin. Simon, the magician-turned-Christian (Acts 8:21-23) was apparently not willing to repent specifically of former lust for power and remained *"bound by iniquity"*. Let me say it again. Even after we commit to faith in Christ we will need to confess our wrong and repent, if we are to be freed from generational and pre-conversion bondages.

Judgments and Generational Sin

Anais Nin once said *"We see things the way we are."* It is true from the perspective of eternity that there are things we cannot see ourselves. We do have blind spots and generational sin can be the cause. Often coming to us in the form of judgments, these are not only the thoughts we think but paradigms that have been sown and passed down from the generation before us. Unless we repent specifically of them, we give way to judgments, and set into motion the law of sowing and reaping. In other words, judgments are lightning conductors for the transferance of strongholds between generations. Blessing others, on the other hand, is a conductor for receiving God's mercy and grace. Both bondage and blessing are brought to fruition through the sowing and reaping law.

The Law of Sowing and Reaping and Generational Sin

Like a small tree that becomes a big tree, sins once small in nature, will increase in the magnitude of the harvest. There is a growth factor of sins as they are passed down the generations. The longer they have existed the bigger they become. As any farmer knows, when seed is sown there is always a proportional multiplication of it to be reaped at harvest time. For example, if you plant a grapefruit seed, you will get grapefruit, though many more than the one grapefruit seed which produced a tree. Conversely, if your tree produces a grapefruit, you can be sure a grapefruit seed was once planted! We reap many good things from our ancestors but we also reap many bad traits.

I remember as a teenager when invitations to parties after work included being invited to drink alcohol. I knew that it was wrong but I would consume a little to "be accepted" among the crowd. Gradually it became clear to me that alcohol had a quick and powerful hold on my life and I wondered why. My whole family abstained from alcohol and from a child I was brought up without it. One day I heard a testimony about an alcoholic who was set free from the power of alcohol. He had struggled against it his whole life until he repented for his own sin and asked God's forgiveness on behalf of his forebears who had fallen into this sin. Finally the power of alcoholism was broken in his life forever.

That day I prayed about my generational inheritance in faith, not being aware then of details of my inheritance. Repenting to God for my own sin and that of my forebears, I also renounced the power of alcoholism over my life and over the generations. I have never had a problem with refusing alcohol since my repentance prayer and now have a strong aversion for it. Later I learned that the disease of alcoholism had been a problem with my maternal grandfather.

In God's legal universe the law of sowing and reaping must be satisfied. Just as my thoughts of acceptance that depended on the need to consume alcohol in public were a lie, a previous generation had been deceived by the same deception — their deficit of God's love. They didn't know they could receive the love they wanted from Father God. Whatever has been sown will be reaped. It's a law that never fails to operate.

The laws of God are laws of the universe. We are dealing with an eternal God who has put eternity in our hearts; whether for heaven or hell does mean a choice. If we are to live in God's blessing there is only one way to go, that is with God. If we have sown kindness and forgiveness, mercy and compassion towards others, the heavenly videos, which can not lie, will tally up and send us the reward. If we have obeyed the Lord, loved Him and His people, then He will crown us with blessing, *pressed down shaken together and running over.* People also, will bless us over and above what we deserve.

Getting Free from the Cycle Whether it is our own sin or generational sin, it will be reaped. As well, the enemy of our souls knows our ignorance about God's laws and will try everything to entangle us. Including historical information, he can use our personal reactions to condemn and ensnare, if possible destroying us before we can repent and put an end to the pattern of sin. Though trailing us may be years of sin baggage, coping mechanisms of rationalisation, demands for justice and blame shifting only keep us in the cycle of judgments. Instead, Father God wants to heal us. He waits to extend His mercy. He waits to hear us let go of injustices and of generational sins, to hear us forgive everybody who has ever done anything to hurt us. The heart change involves becoming aware.

The Compounding Effects of Generational Sin

Knowing a little of how God's laws have been transgressed and the reaping of broken covenants, is to become aware of the compounding of sin. We are corporate in a very real way. Though we may deal individually with isolated situations, we are easily reminded of similar scenarios that are repeated over and over again in contemporary society. Each new generation sows to the future, up to four generations ahead! According to the law of sowing and reaping then, the longer generational sin has existed, the greater the damage and deeper the pattern of evil to be harvested! Isn't this what newspapers are demonstrating as violence and corruption flood society, at ever increasing levels?

Let me give you an example from the Chinese part of the world to demonstrate what I mean by the compounding effects of sin.

Chinese National Woundedness

Speaking of his own people, one Chinese writer said that thousands of years of feudal authoritarian government has:

> *"... crippled our thinking, hampered our judgment, perverted our world view and kept us bottled up inside a set of thick walls. This influence has also impaired our ability to make moral judgments and deprived us of the courage to act on principle. As a result, we can only react to the real world through our emotions and our intuition. In sum, we have*

lost the ability to think straight ....[1] "

Remember, their suffering dates back 4,000 years or more! For a plethora of reasons, the Chinese need healing and love, as we all do! Everybody on the face of the earth needs to have the choice to think God's thoughts. He is the source of real freedom, for His thoughts are truth and they set us free. After being repeatedly told, "Don't bother me!", "Shut up!", "I don't have time for you", "You're good for nothing!", "You're nothing but a slave!" or "You'll never amount to anything", something about creativity dies. Psychologists now tell us that for every negative word a child hears, 40 words of praise are required to remove it!

At times I think God is dealing with our attitudes, especially when we feel exasperated and overwhelmed while making relationships with Chinese. Is He perhaps getting our attention and showing us their brokenness so we will ask the Father to intervene by His love? If what we have just read is true of the need for healing and restoration for individuals even in one generation, how much more so for Chinese people with a long history of many generations who walked in darkness?

A friend of mine compared the need for healing of Chinese history with a bombing in recent years. She was amazed by the wounding and emotional, psychological and societal pain resulting from the terrorist bomb blast that destroyed the Murrah Federal Building in Oklahoma City, USA. In contrast, Bo Yang wrote in 1992 that wars have been a fact of life in every year of Chinese history[2] . This unique perspective on societal distress makes it easy to see how the compounding unresolved pain over generations has likely altered the soul of a people or nation.

---

1 Bo Yang, *The Ugly Chinaman and the Crisis of Chinese Culture* (Malaysia, Allen & Unwin Pty Ltd) p.41

2 Ibid., p. 50

As Bo Yang also intimates, the historical and cultural system of Chinese masters has been a primal source of bondage. It has been handed down for centuries. It is still nurtured and cultivated in the hearts of the young, regardless of what political system is employed. For example, the father image is often driven and demanding, not just with a lust for power but busily reaching to be "the top", or to gain mastery over others. Unresolved father issues abound.[3] Others, through fear of violation, abuse, loss of face, disloyalty and an unwillingness to be known as individuals, blindly adopt ways of past eras. As sins have entangled all of us for generations, though in different ways, the Chinese people typically choose the less confrontational methods, such as tolerance and passivity rather than contemplating the consequences of their actions. Seldom taking a stand on issues, nor expressing an opinion in public unless in a master position, they rarely reveal what they are really thinking and feeling.

As we have seen, the healing of the land *begins* with God's chosen individuals humbling themselves in repentance and prayer. Consider some Biblical examples of how corporate groups of people repented, and how some didn't. We will see now how God dealt with generational sin.

Narratives from the Bible

God takes generational sin seriously, as seen in His wiping out of almost all the human race with the great flood in **Noah**'s time, because of human wickedness. Or, consider the tower of Babel,

---

[3] There are many strains on Chinese families. In ancient China the husband ate before his wife. Today wives can be blamed, mistreated when there is no truth to it. Society and families emphasize IQ but not 'EQ' (emotional intelligence). *"Chinese children are taught that a family problem should not be shared with outsiders. Trust and a relationship must first be developed before an outsider's [counselor's] offer of help or assistance will be welcomed."*.. *Suicide is one of the major problems facing Chinese families.. Suicide is acceptable to many Chinese because of the reincarnation concept taught in Buddhism."* These facts and quotes were taken from *"Ai Jia: Love Your Family"* (Focus on the Family with Dr James Dobson, Coming Home, November 2000, Colordo Springs, USA)

where He confused Nimrod's plans to build his way to heaven (and challenge God's authority)! Since that time the whole world has had to study new tongues to communicate cross-culturally.

On the other hand, the people of **Ninevah** took Jonah's warning seriously. The Bible tells us it was a wicked city and Jonah spared nothing about their coming fate. It was a frank repentance message preached in black and white. Everyone from the greatest to the smallest spent time on their knees, or in the language of their day, *in sackcloth and ashes.* The result? The judgment was averted on that generation and did not come until many years later. God doesn't miss prayers of genuine contrition.

Abraham's conversation with God about **Sodom and Gomorrah** is another example of how the Almighty was willing to spare the city if only for the sake of *ten good men.* The next day though, He took action against the whole generation because not even that many were found. Of course, what God does is always good. His judgment brings cleansing to the earth. When a people has received much warning, yet continually chooses to reject God's right ways, won't there be serious consequences and a reaping of what has been sown?

In Chapter three we noted the scriptural accounts of how **Moses, Stephen and Daniel** took responsibility for generational sins and personally repented and pleaded forgiveness before God on behalf of others. Through prayer they aligned themselves specifically with a section of humanity, then acknowledged the sin, pleaded with God for forgiveness and stated willingness and commitment to change where necessary.

It may seem strange to be confessing sin that neither we nor our ancestors has committed. John Dawson says that "we can all identify with the roots of any given sin." We have all hated at one time, lusted, lied, betrayed, and thought destructive thoughts of others though we may have never physically murdered anyone! Sin is sin and we all rely on God's mercy every day of our lives. We therefore need to remain humble and prayerful toward others in need of mercy.

Other Old Testament prophets **Jeremiah, Nehemiah and Daniel** were among those who confessed their nation's sins, though they were never party to them. They were obeying the instructions received from God in Leviticus 26:40,42.

> *"But, if they confess their iniquity and the iniquity of their fathers, with their unfaithfulness in which they were unfaithful to Me, and that they also have walked contrary to Me.. then I will remember My covenant with Jacob, and My covenant with Isaac and My covenant with Abraham I will remember; I will remember the land"* (NKJV).

The people of Jeremiah and **Ezekiel**'s days complained it was unfair that they should suffer for the sins of others. Since they had been exiled to Babylon, they quoted a proverb that went:

> *..'The fathers eat grapes, and the children's teeth are set on edge' (Ezekiel 18:2 and Jeremiah 31:29).*

In so saying the exiles were suggesting that the reason for their bondage in Babylon was because of their parents' sins and not their own (a form of blame-shifting). The prophets of God each put the record right by saying that a righteous person who turned away from the Lord into iniquity, when they died in it, died because of the iniquity (Ezekiel 18:26). Literally, *"the soul that sins shall die."* Furthermore, if a wicked person turned from his sins, he would live because of the right things he had done (Ezekiel 18:20, Jeremiah 31:29-30). Considering these words, some people say today that Jeremiah and Ezekiel spoke contrary to the covenantal law and reaping of generational sin. Dr Gary S. Grieg, Associate Professor of Old Testament, Regent University, reminds us that shortly after this, both prophets confronted the Judeans with the ongoing reality of generational sins (Jeremiah 32:18 and Ezekiel 20:20-31). They stated specifically what was wrong and Ezekiel paralleled the fathers' sins with the childrens' still going on 'to this day'. The point the prophets now clearly upheld was that only those children who turned and repented for their sins *and* the sins of their fathers would avoid punishment. Jeremiah repented for the generational sin of his fellows (3:25; 14:7, 20). This text supports God's judgment of breaking covenant, that only repentance for our sins and the sins of our fathers breaks the chain reaping of sin.

Generational Styles of Sin

In his excellent book entitled *Healing of the Nations* (Chosen Books), John Sandford cites examples of how generational sin styles have affected nations. He describes how those nations — the religious, political and ethnic groupings — were affected by sins of individual citizens. I have chosen to quote a very clear example which was of great help to liberate a close friend. John Sandford writes:

> *"I could catalog peculiar traits in many nations of the world, but one is outstanding. Australians, like many Americans, are usually warm, open and outspoken. But that nation (as you probably recall) began as a British penal colony, criminal outcasts abused, by some British guards and soldiers. One of the historical results has been a "down-under" mentality, bitter root judgments and expectancies to be abused and regularly given the short end of the stick. In war this has meant that almost invariably they are assigned to suicidal tasks like Gallipoli.*

At Gallipoli during World War I, in the ultimately disastrous Allied expedition to capture the Dardanelles Straits, Australians were ordered to charge uphill against entrenched machine guns, to protect British landings on the beach below. Repeatedly they charged heroically and were mowed down — after which it was discovered that the English had long since landed successfully and were sitting comfortably on the beach having tea. ....

Today, politically and economically, Australians still expect and often receive the same kind of treatment."[4]

These are the consequences of bitter root judgments and expectancies made generations ago. Shirley's inheritance is not strongly Australian. The closest full-blooded tie was an Australian grandfather. As well, her mother had spent her childhood in Australia and my friend's own public education also commenced in the Australian system. Shirley is a strong Christian but nevertheless struggled with cyclical, negative thinking patterns. Upon reading the above account, she could identify with the exact same patterns in her life. Alone with God, she began to repent for judgments she had chosen to retain as passed on from her ancestors. Included in the prayer for whom she asked God's forgiveness were her ancestors. She entreated God that their judgments and dishonoring of the British authorities during the settlement period in Australia's history be forgiven. Then she asked for cleansing by the blood of Jesus, and that the power of these judgments and expectations be broken across the generations. At her prayer group two weeks later, an Australian visitor had a word of knowledge about someone who had suffered from negative, condemnatory and cyclical

---

[4] John Loren Sandford, *"Healing the Nations, A Call to Global Intercession"* (Chosen Books, a division of Baker Book House Company, Grand Rapids, 2000)pp 193-194

thinking. When Shirley responded for prayer, the visitor replied that the word from the Lord had been given for another person. What a gift! From that time she knew that she was free. Perhaps it was no mistake that this quiet declaration of liberty had come from an Australian. Shortly after Shirley noticed a change. With more declarations based on scripture she noticed greater freedom. Good things started happening, like a river without an end! Soon, Shirley felt and experienced God's blessing every day. Old thought patterns were shrugged off. The generational judgments and expectations were broken. God's love towards Shirley had always been the same. It was her own sin and the generational judgments and bitter root expectations which barred her from experiencing the blessing and love of God.

Chinese history We can see in Chinese history how broken covenants and violations of God's laws, judgments and bitter root expectations have sown curses and reaped violence, revenge and murder. Just as in the Australian account, generational sin patterns have become operable at political and economical levels.

Political leaders in ancient China originally governed individual states. The warlords, like small kings, actively protected their land-boundaries and wiped out their opponents and suspect enemies. In the dynasties that followed the first emperor, Qin Shi Huang Di, the royal records were frequently changed or obliterated if the reigning emperor didn't like the previous dynasty. People easily lost their lives. Usually "the country" was the stated as the cause. One example is the Great Wall of China (completed 250 B.C.), which was built at the cost of many lives. Historically, the Chinese and certainly their emperors seemed to display judgments and bitter root expectancies (fears) of being invaded, treated harshly, destroyed and losing their place as the "middle" (or most important) kingdom of the world. A "warring" mind-set developed, an inheritance of destruction.

Perhaps that may be part of war or Chinese culture. Let's look a little closer though at a small section of forty-five years of history. Though the British were not without fault for their heavy demands of reparation which they exacted from the Chinese, there were other causes which led to the Boxer Rebellion in 1900. (Don't both sides contributing to an argument carry responsibility?) In 1899 the Empress Ci Xi planted ploys and encouraged a two month seige of foreigners, so warning of her wish to see them out of Beijing.[5] The Boxer Rebellion began on the heels of the unrest in 1900 by a secret Chinese order. Mostly consisting of young men, they began to murder the native Christians in the countryside and soon surrounded foreign compounds in Beijing and Tianjin. Empress Ci Xi then joined her lot with the Boxers, decreeing war, which became international. We now know that the Boxer Rebellion resulted in 230 missionaries and their children being murdered by the Chinese. More tragic is the statistic that over 32,000 of *the Chinese who were classed Christians*, were annihilated.[6] Many more Chinese died at the hands of their own people, though Christians were often targeted.[7] Their murder was barbaric, involving torture, rape and mutilation.

Japan and China were caught up in the power balancing game that also typified other foreign nations before World War II. Consider however, the Rape of Nanjing, in view of the law of sowing and reaping that never fails. The history of how this war

---

5 Madge Huntington, *A Traveller's Guide to Chinese History* (New York, USA, Henry Holt & Co., 1987) pp 121-124.

6 Robert C. Forsyth, *The China Martyrs of 1900: A Complete Roll of the Christian Heroes Martyred in China in 1900 with Narratives of Survivors* (The Religious Tract Society 1904). E. H. Edwards, *Fire and Sword in Shansi: The Story of the Martyrdom of Foreigners and Chinese Christians* (Oliph and Anderson & Ferrioer, 1903). Of the 32,000 Chinese murdered, 30,000 were Catholic, but 189 of the missionaries killed by Boxers were protestants, the largest such martyrdom in missions history.

7 *The Boxer Rising,*(The American Bible Society, A history of the Boxer trouble in Holds, 1979) p. 7

began is not detailed here,[8] however the outcome interests us. In July 1937 full war broke out between Japan and China and in December, Nanjing, the Chinese capital at that time, was captured. Many locals had already fled the city before the invasion, yet according to historians more than half a million Chinese remained trapped in the city. The Japanese were given the order to kill all captives in Nanjing. *"During the ensuing chaos, commonly referred to as the "Rape of Nanking" between 200,000 and 300,000 or more Chinese lost their lives to Japanese soliders according to court records and historians."*[9] Now the Chinese were mercilessly raped, tortured, mutilated and murdered by the Japanese. Although large numbers of people died, this event and the ensuing reign of the Japanese is remembered particularly for its brutality.

Consider that intercessional repentance is needed for generations of genocide. In the accounts of two wars just presented, the brutality of the conflict emerged along with the cyclical reaping of past bloodshed. Here is a generational sin pattern that can be powerfully addressed by Chinese Christians themselves. In praying through these ancestral sins, won't there be a healing impact? I pray it will not be too late for this cleansing that is so desperately needed.

---

[8] Growing domestic opposition to the Nationalist government policy of self-strengthening before counter attacking in North China and Manchuria led to the kidnapping of Chiang Kai Shek, ... Chiang was forced to agree to a united anti-Japanese front with the communists as a condition for his release. The situation was tense and in 1937 full war commenced. A clash (July, 1937) between soldiers of the Japanese garrison at Beijing and Chinese forces at the Marco Polo Bridge was the pretext for Japanese occupation at Beijing and Tianjin. Chiang Kai Shek refused to negotiate an end to hostilities on Japanese terms and placed crack troops outside the Japanese settlement at Shanghai. After a protracted struggle Shanghai and the national capital, Nanjing, fell to the Japanese in December 1937.. The Columbia Encyclopedia, Sixth Edition, Sino-Japanese War, Second, 2001.

[9] Ami Chen Mills, *Breaking the Silence* (Metro Active News and Issues, The Rape of Nanking, 1996)

Steps to Healing

Change will not come by political decrees, social reforms or committee meetings; these have been applied over and over but to no avail. And the generational cycles of sin have continued far too long. It is time the corporate sin strongholds were given the boot by called, united Spirit-filled warriors.

When people repent, who knows what God can do? The sky is the limit! Harmful tendencies can be arrested, potential wars can dissipate and destructive patterns can be turned around when confronted by the power of the blood of Jesus. As long as repentance to God and an expression of forgiveness are offered between the parties for historical sins, the Holy Spirit will make the rest of the way clear from there. Sharing communion together adds power to the time of repentance. It reminds us that we are in covenant with each other and the Lord.

No course of learning needs to be completed prior to research. It will take individuals or prayer groups who know the power of repentance prayer and the authority invested in them to take the initiative. They must study histories of nations, cities, suburbs, and even families to find the specific roots of sin. Whether first nation people or foreigners, all can be led by God in repentance prayer.

To tip the balance

When the bowls of the saints' intercession overflows the scales of God's mercy will be tipped toward a whole nation. We must keep praying. We who have already received from the sweet fountain of Jesus' blood are covenant-bound to continue in prayer, that soon others may join us and share the grace we enjoy. From seeds of repentance will come a springtime with the rain of His mercy, then a summer, mature fruit and a harvest of corporate repentance.

PRAYER POINTS

• That *many* Chinese Christians will offer repentance to God for the sins of their forebears, declare forgiveness to fellow countrymen and receive healing. *"Come, and let us return unto the Lord: for he has torn so that He may heal us; He has stricken so that He may bind us up*" (Hosea 6:1, AMP). *"Then shall we know, if we follow on to know the Lord: his going forth is prepared as the morning; and he shall come unto us as the rain, as the latter and former rain unto the earth* (Hosea 6:3, AMP)."

• For unity to come to Christ's body in Beijing. *"I have given to them the glory and honor which You have given Me, that they may be one, [even] as We are one: I in them and You in Me, in order that they may become one and perfectly united, that the world may know and [definitely] recognize that You sent Me, and that You have loved them [even] as You have loved Me* (John 17:22,23, AMP)".

Epilogue to the Prayer Strategy

You will be asking if there were other signs of God's intervention after the prayer strategy in Beijing. There were two aspects I wish to cover, in answer to this question. Firstly, let me share a brief history of how the prayer strategy continued between September 1994 and March 1995.

September 1994 to March 1995

During the second term of 1994, we remained in prayer for the city but I relinquished leadership responsibilities to a team of others. (This was in obedience to the Lord and advice from a personal advisor.) The Lord was faithful to speak with visions and prophecies to others about the city. One of those visions is recorded below. We felt it was significantly worded, as it spoke in feminine terms, the opposite of that outlaid in the city plans.

> *"God's plan is for Beijing to be a living symbol of the Bride of Christ, a woman whose virtues and characteristics are: fruitful, peace loving, life giving, efficient and productive. The image of the human body was given in the vision to illustrate that the blood circulation system is to be a model for a plan to spiritually occupy the city. Just as blood flows*

through the body and is the life of the body, so we Christians throughout the city are to be moving and bringing life to her. Believers are to maintain the city in prayer groups, mobilized to keep it clean, even as blood carries away impurities. Likewise, ongoing prayer and fasting are the effective means by which stronghold areas of the city are to be brought down. In this way we act as antibodies in the blood which battle all sickness and disease.

The implications of such a plan and the strong impression felt at the time of the vision was that large numbers of believers are to be involved in the whole process."

The leaders of the prayer strategy, in response to this vision therefore, mapped out the city by its seven innercity administrative districts; HaiDian, FengTai, ChaoYang, ChongWen, XuanWu, XiCheng and DongCheng. Individuals located in those districts volunteered a specific prayer commitment. We did make more prayer visits, the most notable of which was to the gates of the city.

Prayer Visit to Gates of the City

Twelve pairs of prayers visited the eleven gates which had been designated parts of the demon god's body, and the Rostrum at the northern end of Tiananmen Square was the twelfth gate. Pray-ers who had been part of the first term of prayer in 1994 had heard about the Father's love for Beijing being similar to His deep love for Jerusalem. Now further study revealed a correlation between the twelve gates of Jerusalem and those in Beijing. As the Beijing gate names were translated we found counterparts for each one, except for the praise gate, which was missing! Blessings of the Jerusalem gates were matched and prayed over those in Beijing, along with peace and prosperity as worded in Psalms 122, 24 and 48.

Early Snow

While concluding our prayer time at the gates we were caught unprepared, in falling snow. Following later discussion we realised the snow had started falling at 2.00 P.M. precisely, our agreed starting time. One of the team members testified that when he first noticed the snow, he asked the Lord to blanket the city with snow if this was indeed a sign from God of His honoring our prayer. In fact, the snow began falling from Tiananmen Square at the Rostrum, and snow spread to the uttermost parts of the city. Unseasonally heavy, the news of its fall made front-page headlines. The English Edition of the China Daily on November 14 stated it had been unpredicted. It fell so early on November 13, that it was two days before the switch-on date for city-wide heating, November 15!

The prayer strategy leaders organised further prayer visits to places within the city. They included another visit to the Lama Temple and other monastic schools of learning, some newspaper companies and CCTV.

The second aspect of God's intervention in the city is testimony to our prayers.

What Has Happened Since

Of course, the most obvious things which happened, were the breaking of the drought and the collapse of the Dragon Pavillion. Those were mentioned in Chapter Six as direct answers from God. Also appropriate is an update on the summer rainfall in the years from 1994 to 2000. According to local Beijing residents, the rainfall amounts were significantly more following, than in years previous to 1994. Whereas in 1994 it rained nearly every day, the summer rainfall was considerable for each of the intervening years until 2000. Locals in the province surrounding Beijing, Hebei, also spoke of huge downpours of rain in the years following 1994.

A small, yet not insiginificant surprise awaited us. Two men of God who had visited Beijing frequently prior to the first half of 1994, visited again in September and October. They had more than a passing appreciation of the spiritual concerns of the city. Unknown to each other, they commented independently to us on a change they had noticed in the spiritual atmosphere of the city. They asked us what had happened in Beijing? In particular they identified the friendly, open manner of taxi drivers in contrast to what they had experienced before. (Taxi drivers are one group we foreigners generally have much contact with.) I believe the sign of open friendliness was a reflection of our repentance for the walls we had built among each other and in the city (see the repentance prayer at the beginning of Chapter 5). Reflect on this witness to change by Christians who had not known of our prayer for the city.

Consider the following as a work of God and a result of our repentance. In April 1995, the exposure of a major corruption scandal was reported to the public. The huge amount of $2.2 billion embezzled by Mayor Li and the Communist Party leader Chen Xitong finally became too big for cover. A jealous wife spoke up. It took two years for resolution of the matter but these two were later evicted from the Party and sentenced to prison in September 1997. Corruption has since been admitted by the Party heads as a major problem which threatens the authority of the Communist Party. There was also a five year crack-down on party members which began in the mid-1990's resulting in 121,500 people being dismissed. Much prayer both prior and following the publication of the corruption scandal is something I can vouch for. As part of our prayer for the city, *we had corporately repented for engaging in idolatry, for courting control and being driven by lust and control* (see the repentance prayer in Chapter Five). The problem of corruption, a fruit of idolatry and desire to control financially, is nowhere near solved. Is not, however, the exposure of sin at high levels of government a work of God?

The End of the Prayer Strategy

In March, 1995, the group which met to carry out the prayer strategy officially disbanded. In obedience to the Lord to enter into rest, I had been slowly withdrawing my involvements with the prayer strategy. Some found my decision to withdraw hard to handle, though others formed a core group as they feld led of the Holy Spirit to work together. Early in the second term, in September of 1994, I completely withdrew from the leadership and decision-making body. My involvement did become less as time went on and by December 1994 this process was complete. I had heard the call to write by then and so made an announcement that I was out of circulation for that purpose. However, it had taken me longer than it should have to exit. If I had withdrawn much sooner some mistakes could have been avoided. Some months later, in March 1995, the majority decided on another direction and the group meetings as they had been known ended. We later shared communion and in the process expressed love to each other.

I believe the Holy Spirit's main purpose for the 1994 prayer group had been completed. However, the call to prayer to the body of Christ is ongoing, something which the International Fellowship later recognised in 1998, by it's annual designation of the month of April to prayer and fasting for the city. As well, many international prayer teams from many countries have come to Beijing. The Holy Spirit has shown us that prayer is consistently needed for Beijing!

The scriptures celebrate that Elijah didn't give up until he got what he was praying for (James 5:16,17). Neither should we! In April 1998, the season of prayer for Beijing culminated with two international churches forgiving each other. On that day, it was taught that God's progression to answering Elijah's prayer was from nothing, to a small cloud, to abundance of rain. We were admonished to pray expectantly, earnestly and continually for our city. The battle is not over and we have the Victor on our side. Let's use our weapons effectively and take up God's call to win!

Appendixes

APPENDIX A: Example Prayers

Repentance for Idolatry

• God, please forgive and cleanse us from idolatry. We repent for defiling Your land, the land You gave us. Forgive us for filling Your inheritance with the images of our detestable and abominable idols, for profaning and mocking Your Name, O God. Have mercy, Lord and cleanse us, all that we own, and the lands of our inheritance from the curse of our own disobedience (From Jeremiah 16:18).

Repentance for Immorality and Fornication

• Forgive us Lord, for sexual indecency and uncovering the nakedness of others and ourselves. As a people we admit unfaithfulness in and before marriage. Lord God, we confess homosexuality, and lesbianism and bestiality. We have turned our hearts from you. We acknowledge our sin publicly. Please forgive and cleanse us and our land from the curse of our sins (From Leviticus 18:1-23).

Repentance for Broken Covenants

• Forgive us Father, in Jesus name for breaking the laws of Your Word, and for living without regard to your Covenant. We confess that we have broken promises toward friends, our family, our community, city and the nation (Be specific!). We invite you to take up first place in our hearts and lives, to be Lord and Master of our inheritances, of our families, of our homes, suburbs and city. Restore to us the right paths and the grace to observe your laws and help us to live in Your ways until You come again. O God, forgive us and cleanse us with the blood of Jesus in Jesus' name because we have respect for Your Word. Break the curse from our land and off our people by the blood of Jesus in Jesus' name.

Repentance for Bloodshed

• O Father, in Jesus' name, forgive us and our ancestors for aborting our children. We confess the murder of innocent children within and outside the womb, that we have selfishly silenced life that You gave, and we have not listened to the cries of the innocent. Forgive us for profaning Your name in this way. Forgive us Lord, for defiling the land and polluting it, especially for murder, mass slaughter of others and all the planning that has approved those actions. God in Heaven, please cleanse our fingers from this great sum of terrible iniquity and cleanse our hands from defilement. Please Jesus, cleanse our lips, mouths and bodies from lies when we have covered our sin. Forgive us, O God, for murdering your servants and prophets, those who prayed for us even while we killed them! O God, have mercy and forgive, cleanse our land of defilement by the blood of Jesus in the name of Jesus, according to the promise of Your Word.

More Scriptures to use in prayer for Beijing

• *Yes, all kings* (in Beijing) *shall fall down before Him; All* nations (including Beijing) *shall serve Him. For He will deliver the needy when he cries* (in Beijing), *The poor also, and him who has no helper* (in Beijing). *He* (You, O God) *will redeem their life from oppression and violence; And precious shall be their blood in His sight.* (Psalm

72:11-14, NKJV), (words added for emphasis).

• *The Lord builds up Jerusalem;* (Beijing); *He gathers together the outcasts of Israel;* (China). *He heals the brokenhearted And binds up their wounds... Great is our Lord, and mighty in power; His understanding is infinite. The Lord lifts up the humble* (in Beijing); *He casts the wicked down to the ground* (Psalm 147:2,3,5,6, NKJV), (words added for emphasis).

• *All the kings of the earth* (including Beijing's) *shall praise You, O Lord, When they hear the words of Your mouth. Yes, they shall sing of the ways of the Lord, For great is the glory of the Lord. Though the Lord is on high, Yet He regards the lowly; But the proud He knows from afar* (Psalm 138:4-6, NKJV), (words added for emphasis).

• *O Lord, make bare Your holy arm before the eyes of all the nations. Reveal Yourself as the One by whose direction the redemption of* (Beijing) *from captivity is accomplished. Let all the ends of the earth witness the salvation of our God* (Isaiah 52:10, amp), (words added for emphasis).

• *Help us, O God of our salvation, For the glory of Your name; And deliver us, and provide atonement for our sins, For Your name's sake! Why should the nations say, "Where is their God?" Let there be known among the nations in our sight The avenging of the blood of Your servants which has been shed. Let the groaning of the prisoner come before You; According to the greatness of Your power Preserve those who are appointed to die; And return to our neighbors sevenfold into their bosom Their reproach with which they have reproached You, O Lord. So we, Your people and sheep of Your pasture, Will give You thanks forever; We will show forth Your praise to all generations* (Psalm 79:9-13 NKJV), (words added for emphasis).

• *Why do the nations* (China) *rage, And the people plot a vain thing? The kings of the earth set themselves, And the rulers take counsel together, Against the Lord and against His Anointed, saying "Let us break Their bonds in pieces And cast away Their cords from us." He who sits in the heavens shall laugh; The Lord shall hold them in derision* (Psalm 2:1-4, NKJV), (words added for emphasis).

- *"Let the high praises of God be in their* (my) *throat and a two-edged sword in their* (my) *hand, To wreck vengeance upon the* (your) *nations and chastisements upon the* (your) *peoples; To bind their* (your) *kings with chains and their* (your) *nobles with fetters of iron, To execute upon them* (you) *the judgment written. He* [the Lord] *is the honor of all His saints. Praise the Lord! Hallelujah*! (Psalm 149:6-9, amp), (words added for emphasis).

APPENDIX B: Authority for Intercession

• God's authority given to man: *'Then God blessed them, and God said to them, "Be fruitful and multiply; fill the earth and subdue it; have dominion over the fish of the sea, over the birds of the air, and over every living thing that moves on the earth"'* (Genesis 1:28, NKJV).

• Jesus came to undo the works of the devil (1 John 3:8) and re-established our authority to remit the sins of others: *'If you forgive the sins of any, they are forgiven them; if you retain the sins of any, they are retained'* (John 20:23, NKJV).

• We have authority over all the power of the enemy: *'"Behold, I give you the authority to trample on serpents and scorpions, and over all the power of the enemy, and nothing shall by any means hurt you"'* (Luke 10:19, NKJV).

• We have authority to overcome the devil: *'And they overcame him by the blood of the Lamb and by the word of their testimony, and they did not love their lives to the death'* (Revelation 12:11, NKJV).

• We have authority to intercede for the land as God calls us: *'So I sought for a man among them who would make a wall, and stand in the gap before Me on behalf of the land, that I should not destroy it; but I found no one'* (Ezekiel 22:30, NKJV).

• We have God's authoritative promise for cleansing from our sin, when we confess it to God, personally and corporately: *'If we confess our sins He is faithful and just to forgive us our sins and to cleanse us from all unrighteousness'* (1 John 1:9, NKJV).

APPENDIX C: Seven Sentinels for Prayer Sentries

"Be strong [confident], and of good courage, for you shall cause this people to inherit the land, which I swore to their fathers to give them.... Have not I commanded you? Be strong, vigorous and very courageous; be not afraid, neither be dismayed; for the Lord your God is with you wherever you go." (Joshua 1:6,9,AMP).

Now that Moses had gone Joshua was being given leadership at a critical time. He would not only take them into the promised land, he would cause the Israelites to *inherit* their land. This process of inheriting turned out to be more than just receiving that inheritance, but fighting for and taking over ownership responsibility for the apportioned land. Joshua taught the tribes to reclaim land *themselves.*

The people God has called and equipped to lead us in bringing city-wide transformation are unknown and faceless, but they have big hearts and big visions. God makes them known only because of their obedience to Him. These people may not even think of themselves as leaders but they need to be encouraged to listen at heart-level to that call and to step out. Some may be pastors, but on the other hand, they may be mothers or fathers in the Kingdom who have God-given ability (and so authority) to bring unity in the city among God's people. Such leaders train others in proactive spiritual warfare and in reclaiming lost ground *themselves*. No one leader has an exclusive right to spiritual warfare! On the contrary, it is only when everyone stands for his or her *own* area that a large city can be covered. Let's look at some sentinels or trumpet calls that as prayer sentries, we can be prepared to hear along the road to change.

Sentinel 1) The call to Sign-up There will be a call to believing faith that God can *use me,* in prayer for a city. That call, for *whomever will* to get involved, if handled correctly, will require us each hearing from God for *ourselves. Getting* to hear from God may mean dealing with our own stronghold mindsets.

We need a resolute prayer attitude. To see the will of God for a city established is possible because His word says *nothing* is impossible with God (Luke 1:37). The adversary of our souls would like us to believe something that is not the will of God to confine our faith and to keep us praying petty prayers that don't pass the ceiling! When we believe something contrary to God's will, that is a choice for a stronghold mindset, and it is a mind without hope. Other issues may arise such as how we deal with criticism, the ability to give love unconditionally and letting go lies of fear or deception. How desperate are we for God to come — enough to get right with Him?

There needs to be transformation in our hearts before there can be change in the city! I would say too though, that having answered the call to prayer, God will equip. Don't expect a heart transplant before sign-up! On the contrary, we can begin to dance on the land God has given us right now! We must be ready to move outside our conceived boundaries to receive His limitless victory in the city.

Sentinel 2) The call to Mapping Boundaries — Spiritual mapping, as we have discussed is simply asking what the root of the problem is. We need to know what to ask God for, to be in touch with the personality of the city and the forces operating for good and evil. If we ask aright, God will answer our prayers! Wise and faithful warriors do intelligence operations to learn about the city. Sure trusteeship of the land will mean understanding the intrinsic nature of the city, where boundaries have been violated, where the gates no longer function and where the walls no longer keep bad out and good in. The history of the church in the area is an important aspect, as also are the history of wars and treaties (how they were made), a general economic overview, natural disasters and any repetitive patterns linked to the city. Has the occult been used to decide location and planning? How were the first nation peoples treated by foreigners? All of this is what clarifies our prayer strategies and future outlook. I recommend John Dawson's books for reference and further study (See Appendix F).

If we are praying for the Kingdom of God to come in a specific location, then we should be able to plot where those boundaries lie physically. Don't we pray for the kingdom of God to come in *this* or *that* place and be *among* us? Prayer for cities means staking a definite claim to the people and their land for God, clear-cut and distinguished from the boundaries the devil has claimed. While proclaiming our God-given claims based on His Word, we therefore become specific. That is why, mapping the land, getting to know what exists in our "space" and walking over it for both intelligence and prayer, is part of driving in our stake of spiritual stewardship. We must know what we are committed to! And God may require of us a lengthy term in carrying out our duty there.

Sentinel 3) Call to Strategise — When the city has been

researched (which takes *time),* a definitive vision for the prayer strategy must be put in place. As any general knows, strategy is the factor that wins the war. Whether a city-wide, nation-wide or suburb-based operation, the same is true. The most important thing is that you know for sure that the strategy you have is from God.

The Israelites won battles with a number of approaches, but when they did, it was because they had asked the Lord "if" they were to go up to battle, and if so, "how" they were to do it. I love the Bible battle stories, especially the unconventional approaches. The Bible accounts of them teach us spiritual principles.

Sending the singers and worshippers out front of the army into battle in Jehoshaphat's day sent confusion into the enemy ranks. They just had to stand still, and see God's victory while the enemy soldiers killed each other. In possessing Jericho the Israelites simply walked around the walls six times on six days and seven times on the last day. They were not allowed to speak a word as they walked. Perhaps God was so specific because He knew the Israelites' tendency to negativity, that this would have destroyed faith, and faith was needed to overcome the world at Jericho. Consider that God's intention in all of these varying approaches was to cause defeat in the spiritual realm and He therefore led His people in the opposite spirit to the prevailing powers.

Don't compare your situation with others. It is encouraging and inspiring to hear testimonies of how others have broken through. We can learn much from each other, but only God knows the prevailing demonic powers in your area and how to defeat them. Get the strategy from God. Step by step, He will lead on to victory.

Sentinal 4) Call to Identificational Repentance — As we have discussed, this vital and decisive intercession means recognising and taking responsibility to repent for the historical sins of the people, and to pray for the cleansing of the land. How does answering this call help us take responsibility? It honors the truth that God limits what will go on with His property and the people He created. Only Jesus could die, but only the Body of Christ can take up this priestly function of identificational intercession to bring forgiveness and healing.

We catalogue ourselves with others, *in order to repent,* to truly plead mercy from God, with real contrition of heart. Feelings are important, a key to being real. That is why, when confessing historical sins, allowing emotions to rise to the surface may be what defines a moment. You may remember in Chapter 2 how Salome received a picture from God of a soldier smashing a baby against a wall. It helped her repent *with tears.* Though almost 700 or so years separated her from the days of Mongolian rule, I believe it was effectual repentance.

Historical sins should be well-researched and presented clearly, with no mincing of words. Godly sorrow then has a chance to form within us, until as *we* become actively involved in confession and reconciliation with others, a burden lifts, or a breakthrough comes. Celebrating the release affirms and strengthens it.

Sentinel 5) Call to Persistance and Holy Boldness — When I think about the work of confession of sin, repentance and reconciliation in my own life I cannot put an end to it. This one thing I know, *"I press on to take hold of that for which Christ took hold of me"* (Philippians 3:12, AMP). And, though my confession of sin may not resolve the heart issue immediately, it is a start. Similarly, the healing of the land requires our persistence and perseverance. When an issue arises in our lands it is a cue for fasting and prayer. We must keep going until there is breakthrough!

Holy boldness is being returned to the church. David and Goliath is one Bible battle that exemplifies this. A young man, perhaps in his late teens, witnessed the mockery of the God of the Israelite army. Horrified that *anyone* had dared to defy the armies of the living God, David was even more amazed to find that no one had stood up to this Goliath. Even worse they were afraid, numbed to inaction. David must have known where his questions would take him. In response to his brothers, other soldiers, captains and even the king, David never backed down. He had proved His God, alone, against a lion and a bear. The Almighty was faithful and dependable and David held respect for the One He worshipped, more than anything he feared. He dared *not* allow this humiliation of God's people and His name to continue. So it was that David arose through the ranks and finding none to join him in the Israelite army, challenged the enemy alone. Quoting the name of the Most High God as his authority David felled the giant — the enemy's pawn — with a single pebble. It just took the Lord God and one good, bold man. God needs intercessors with holy boldness today!

Sentinel 6) A call to Change that comprises pain — We have to believe testimonies and answers to prayer, otherwise why do we pray? However, the road ahead is not always easy. Recall what was said earlier, that if the lands are not healed they will defile the dwellers. We read in Romans 8, 19 and 21 how creation is groaning for emancipation from bondage! The release of the creation to freedom is preceded by the maturing of the sons of God. We need to grow sufficiently for the truth of our sonship to be broadcasted, exhibited and shown to impact reality. And that will take some change in us.

The idea of sonship has often fostered the belief that Father is a God who will do everything for us. On one hand, it's true. We must trust our Father to do many things. On the other hand, Jesus told his disciples that a time would come when they would ask and receive directly from the Father. He went on to say:

> *"At that time you will ask (pray) in My name, and I am not saying that I will ask the Father on your behalf [for it will*

be unnecessary]" (John 16:26, AMP).

I believe Jesus was referring to intimacy with the Father that He had and His disciples would have — actually the unfolding of full sonship. Most will agree that a sure sign of adulthood is a person who begins to take responsibility for their lives in a reliable way. Maturity is taking the consequences for sin honestly, then getting needs met by one's own iniative. Part of establishing the freedom that comes with adulthood means staking out our spiritual and emotional space. This process can be painful, though more freedom is the result.

Likewise, intercessors for the nations should be aware of the costly process ahead. As we expose historical sin and begin to confess our sin with contrition of heart, then stand and do warfare, staking out His standards and truths as applying to the nation, there is a price to pay. Through it all, we will grow in many ways and growth means pain. In taking on the God-given mandate though, consider the likely fruit. Perhaps ours was a race that once contributed violence to the earth. Now as children of the Most High God, we seek reconciliation and healing for the depraved inheritance. What could be a more powerful destiny? Today's victories will contribute to our eternal inheritance when we rule and reign with Him (Revelation 2:26,27).

Sentinel 7) Call to Proclamation of God's Word — Many aspects are profoundly important in a prayer strategy: worship, unity and ultimate conquest to name a few. How do we pray, though? Proclaiming God's Word, in prayer and testimony is a major key. What are the words of prophecy which have been given specifically for the city and nation? Which scriptures have been quickened?

Prophecy stimulates our faith and inspires us to do God's will confidently. The declaration of God's Word also guides and empowers our prayer. Just as in Nehemiah's day the builders held their weapons in one hand and built with the other, fierce battles will require our effective use of the Sword of the Spirit, the Word of God, *while we work*. We claim Covenant promises through Jesus blood.

The testimony of how God saved Daniel from the lions was one that changed a heathen king's heart and led to a complete shift of laws pertaining to worship in the land. I love Daniel's fortitude and stamina. The source of his courage and the reason for the breakthrough would have come from his habit of prayer three times a day, when He reminded God of His Word. It's true that we cannot nullify the evil decisions and choices of men but as we continue to declare God's promises, the angels will obey His words that *we* pray (Psalm 103: 20,21). Consistent prayer does bring change in the spiritual realm. When more evidences of the power of God are circulated, people may suddenly decide to follow God. As in Daniel's case, a nation-wide publication of the testimony seals the spiritual breakthrough we have won in prayer (See Daniel 9:20-23 and 10:9-14).

APPENDIX D: Beijing City Maps
The City Walls and Gates of Old Beijing[1]

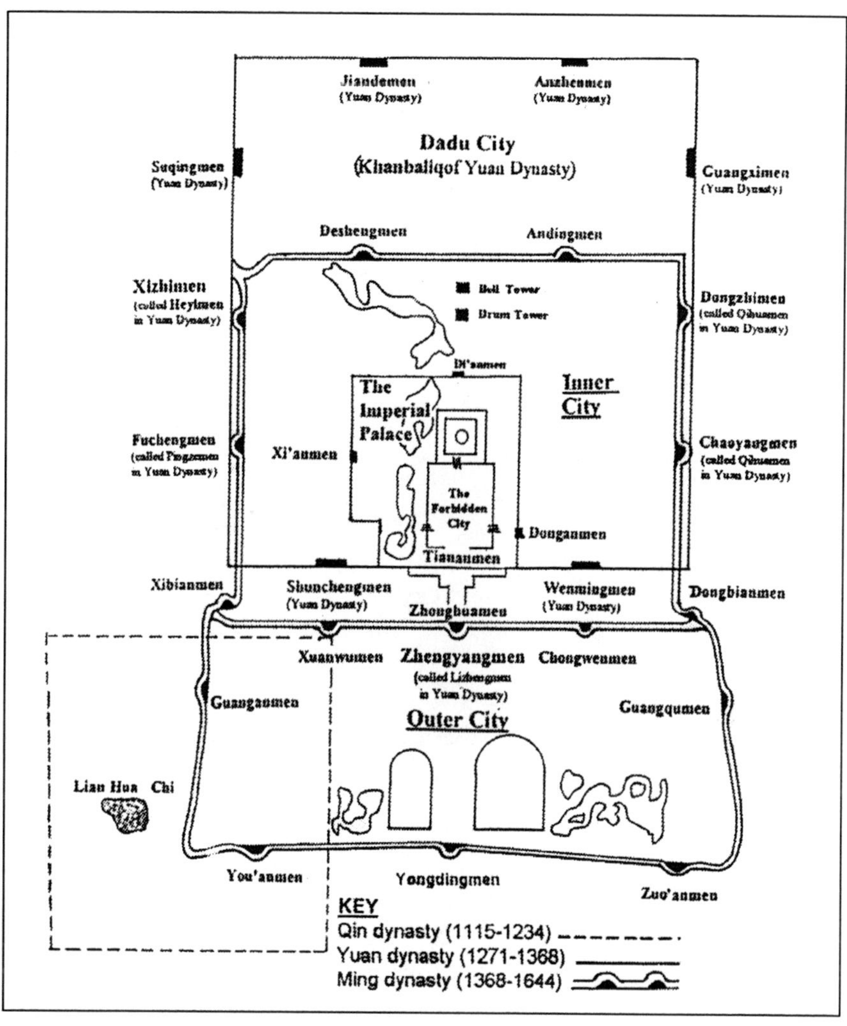

[1] This map was compiled from three sources: L.C. Arlington and William Lewisohn, *In Search of Old Peking* (Hong Kong, Oxford University Press, 1935, 1987); Hedda Morrison, *A Photographer in Old Beijing* (New York, USA, University Press, 1985, 1993); Edited and Compiled by Qi Fang and Qi Jirang, *Old Peking, The City and It's People* (Hong Kong, Hai Feng Publishing Co., 1993).

Places Designated "body parts" of the demon god ne zha[2]

On June 12, 1994 every one of these places was visited and prayed over. Communion was shared and prayer was made for God's purposes to be released in each location. We applied oil, as a symbol of the Holy Spirit's work, and our agreement with His work was made in prayer. The north/south axis which ran for 8 kilometres from Gulou to the Temple of Heaven was cut and severed in prayer by faith in the blood of Jesus in the name of Jesus, as many times as we crossed it during the day. See next page for inset.

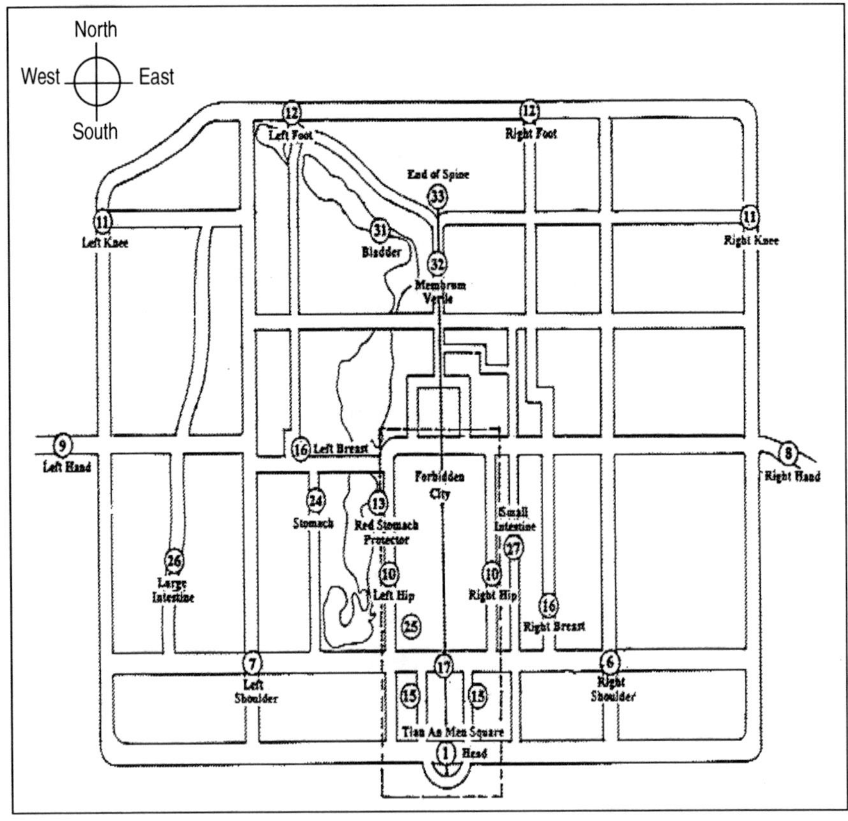

2 This map was based on information divulged from the book authored by L.C. Arlington and William Lewisohn, *In Search of Old Peking* (Hong Kong, Oxford University Press, 1935, 1987).

Places designated "body parts" of the demon god ne zha, listed below

Inset: Forbidden City and Tinanmen Square (Enlarged)

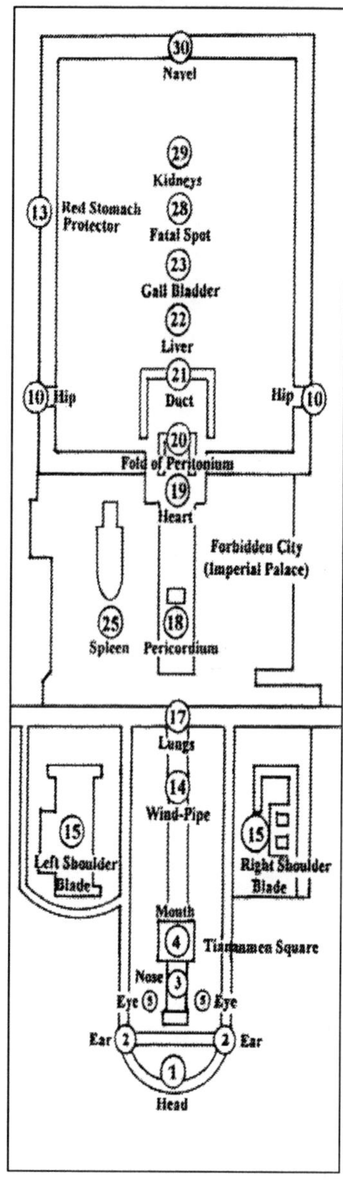

1. Head	Qianmen
2. Ears	Two sides of Qianmen
3. Nose	Area between Qianmen and Mao's Memorial Hall
4. Mouth	Mao's Memorial Hall
5. Eyes	Two wells south of Mao's Memorial
6. Right Shoulder	Chongwenmen (Methodist Church)
7. Left Shoulder	Xuanwumen (Catholic Church)
8. Right Hand	Chaoyangmen
9. Left Hand	Fuchengmen Baitaisi Temple
10. Right & Left Hips	Dunghuamen & Xihuamen East & west gates of Forbidden City
11. Right & Left Knee	Dongzhimen & Xizhimen
12. Right & Left Foot	Andingmen & Deshengmen
13. Red Stomach Protector	Red walls of Forbidden City
14. Wind-pipe	"Imperial Way" - n/s line between Qianmen & Tiananmen
15. Right & Left Shoulder blades	Great Hall of the People & Museum of the Chinese People's Cultural Revolution
16. Breasts	Dunganmen & Xi'anmen
17. Lungs	Tiananmen & space in front
18. Pericordium	By Tiananmen & Duanmen
19. Heart	Wumen
20. Fold of Peritonium	Gate of supreme harmony
21. Duct - connects heart & liver	Hall of supreme harmony
22. Liver	Hall of complete harmony
23. Gall Bladder	Hall of preserving harmony
24. Stomach	3 seas – south, central, north
25. Spleen	Altar of Land and Grain
26. Large Intestine	Zhaodengyu Road & Taiping Road
27. Small Intestine	Beiheyan Street & Nanheyan Street
28. Fatal Spot	Gate of heavenly purity
29. Kidneys	Hall of heavenly purity
30. Navel	A well situated inside Shenwumen (NW wall of Forbidden City)
31. Bladder	Hou hai
32. Membrum Verile	A bridge
33. End of spine	Gulou – Drum Tower/Bell Tower
(34. An altar	Forbidden City)

APPENDIX E:
Prayer Strategy Time Line 1994

Feb	20	Esther handed book *In Search of Old Peking*
March	01	Mary arrived in Beijing
April	09	First visit to Altar of Land and Grain
	16	Visit to Altar of Heaven
	17	First Group Meeting
	24	Second Group Meeting
May	08	Third Group Meeting, Sins of our forefathers (many nations)
	15	Visit to Altar of Sun
	22	Fourth Group Meeting
	28	Visits to Altar of Moon and Altar of Earth
	29	Fifth Group Meeting - Repentance for sins of Chinese
June	04	Visit to Altars of Agriculture, Hills and Streams
	05	Sixth Group Meeting
	11	Day of Prayer — indoors
	12	The Gideon Day — outdoors
July	01	Afternoon of Prayer
	02	Visit to Lama Temple
	03	Rained ALL DAY
	13	Drought Broke
	15	Newspaper printed statement that drought had been broken.
	15	Dragon Temple in Kaifeng collapsed, 1:00 p.m.

APPENDIX F: Recommended Reading

C.P. Wagner	Warfare Prayer	(Regal Books)
	Prayer Shield	(Regal Books)
	Breaking Strongholds in your City	(Regal Books)
	Churches That Pray	(Regal Books)
	Engaging the Enemy	(Regal Books)
Cindy Jacobs	Possessing the Gates of the Enemy	(Chosen Books)
	The Voice of God	(Regal Books)
George Otis, Jr.	The Twilight Labyrinth	(Chosen Books)
John Loren Sandford	Healing the Nations	(Chosen Books)
John Dawson	Taking our Cities for God	(Creation House)
	What Christians Should Know About Reconciliation	(Sovereign World)

Address for ordering of books:
oneagles2u@hotmail.com

CPSIA information can be obtained at www.ICGtesting.com
Printed in the USA
BVOW07s1151080714

358479BV00002B/330/A

9 781931 232647